CONTENTS

The Super Bowl 6
Tom Brady led the drive, Adam Vinatieri made the kick. Champions. Again.

The playoffs 24
In the cold and snow at Foxborough, the Patriots proved to be the AFC's hottest team.

The season 32
After a slow start, the Patriots went unbeaten at home and won 12 in a row with a variety of styles.

The key figures 96
From the coach to the quarterback and positions in between, the Patriots had the right mix of personalities.

BOOK STAFF

Editor Reid Laymance
Designer Rena Anderson Sokolow
Photo editor Jim Wilson
Copy editor Mike Kilduff
Photo Research Theresa Grenier
Special Thanks Alex Teng

The Boston Globe

AGAIN!

THE 2003 PATRIOTS AND THEIR SECOND SUPER SEASON

PANTHERS

HOUSTON

32-29

NE CAR

FEBRUARY 1
2004

INDOORS

All over again

by DAN SHAUGHNESSY

Yogi Berra would have called it, "Deja vu all over again."

It was all so familiar . . . Adam Vinatieri kicking the game-winner . . . quarterback Tom Brady winning the Most Valuable Player Award . . . coach Bill Belichick and owner Bob Kraft hoisting the Vince Lombardi Trophy while Patriot players hugged and brushed confetti off one another. All of these things happened two years ago when the Patriots upset the St. Louis Rams in New Orleans.

After the Patriots had beaten Carolina, 32-29, in Houston for their second Super Bowl in three years, Kraft told the crowd, "Fifty-three players, 17 coaches, a head coach—the heart and soul of our team showed us what the concept of team is all about."

FIRST DOWNS	RUSHING YARDS	PASSING YARDS	TURNOVERS
NE 29｜17 CAR	127｜92	354｜295	1｜1

IT'S UP
Adam Vinatieri's
41-yard field
goal was right
down the middle
and good to give
the Patriots the
win with four
seconds left.

SACKS	PENALTIES	TIME OF POSSESSION	OPPONENTS RECORD
4|0	8|12	38:58|21:02	17-2|14-6

FUMBLE
Mike Vrabel, who
would later score
on offense,
knocks the ball
out of Carolina
quarterback Jake
Delhomme's
hands.

Championships are like children—you love each one equally. But the manner in which the 2003-04 Patriots went about their business makes this title a slightly favored son. The Patriots finished the season with 15 consecutive wins, went 10-0 against winning teams, and went 10 weeks without trailing in a game before the Panthers put them on the ropes at Reliant Stadium.

As ever, Brady was Joe Montana-cool under pressure. With the game tied and a little more than a minute to play, he moved the Patriots 37 yards in six plays, setting up Vinatieri's 41-yard kick for the win with four seconds left. The clutch kicker had missed a 31-yard chip shot, and had another attempt blocked, but his final boot was straight and true.

"Maybe a little deja vu of two years ago," said Vinatieri. "The fellows moved the ball downfield and we had the opportunity to win it again. This never gets old. With this type of venue and the pressure on, it's never easy, but you try to block all the external things out and kick it. I'll cherish this for a long time."

Meanwhile, what's left for Brady? John Kerry's running mate? First man on Mars? Starting pitcher for the Red Sox when they finally win a World Series? The 26-year-old golden child becomes the youngest two-time Super Bowl-winning quarterback and one of only four players to win the MVP Award twice. He completed 32 of 48 passes for 354 yards and three touchdowns. He is 6-0 lifetime in playoff games.

"The guys made some great catches there on that last drive," said Brady. "And Adam drove that sucker right down the middle to win it. What a game. Fitting for the Super Bowl, I guess."

When the Patriots trailed for the first time since before Thanksgiving, Brady moved them 68 yards on 11 plays and regained the lead with a 1-yard touchdown pass to linebacker Mike Vrabel. When the Panthers roared back to tie the game, Brady responded again.

"It was an awesome year," said Belichick. "I can't say enough about the players. We finished the game with two backup safeties. That's the way it's been all year."

So now it's Groundhog Day, where the scene keeps repeating itself, much like in the Bill Murray movie, but there's no one left to beat. Too bad. Patriots fans surely would embrace six more weeks of football. In the wake of the coldest January since 1888, and the most disappointing Red Sox finish since 1986, New England needed a lift, and the Patriots delivered with a season for the ages.

In the end, the Super Bowl win was like so many others in this magical Patriots season. The Patriots failed to overwhelm their opponents, relied on strong defense, got contributions from the entire roster, and left it to Brady and Vinatieri to come through at the finish. The fact that New England's final touchdown pass was caught by a linebacker tells you much of what you need to know about this team.

By any measure, these Patriots go into the books as one of the best and most beloved Boston sports teams of the last 100 years. Not since the Larry Bird Celtics of 1984 and '86 has a local team won two championships in three seasons. The Bruins last did it in 1970 and '72 and the Red Sox haven't turned the trick since 1916 and '18.

The 2003-04 Patriots featured one of the best defenses in league history, used 42 different starters, had only two Pro Bowlers, and took pride in selflessness and interchangeable parts. At times, it looked as if they had 11 coaches on the field. They transformed their two-year-old stadium into the happiest place on earth.

The camaraderie of the Patriots was evident at the start again. Troy Brown, the senior Patriot in continuous service, led the AFC champions onto the field. And as they did two years ago, the Patriots poured out of their tunnel en masse—a show of unity that was copied by the Panthers. It was clear at this moment that the Super Bowl would be like another home game for Belichick's team. Patriot Nation made its presence felt and there were moments when Reliant Stadium sounded like the football theater off Route 1 in Foxborough.

It started out like a World Cup game and was still 0-0 with a little more than three minutes to play in the first half. But Brady threw a pair of touchdown passes in the final three minutes and Carolina's Jake Delhomme started to move his team and New England led, 14-10, at intermission.

After a ribald halftime show featuring Janet Jackson, play was interrupted briefly when a streaker managed to line up with the Panthers for the opening kickoff. He was chased by authorities and eventually brought down when Patriots linebacker Matt Chatham put a shoulder into him. Needless to say, Belichick was not amused.

It got wild again after a scoreless third quarter. The teams traded touchdowns early in the fourth. After a Brady interception, the Panthers struck again on the longest play from scrimmage in Super Bowl history, an 85-yard pass from Delhomme to Muhsin Muhammad. Carolina led, 22-21, with 6:53 left.

Brady went to work and it was madness the rest of the way. As always, the Patriots came through in the clutch.

No doubt there will be whispers of "dynasty." The well-managed, brilliantly coached Patriots are in position to make it back to the national stage in Jacksonville next year.

THE LEGACY

Simply the best

by MICHAEL HOLLEY

IT IS NOW OK TO PLACE THE NEW ENGLAND Patriots in a historical sentence that few teams are able to utter. You can call them one of the greatest teams of all time, and you can say it without apologizing or blinking or giving a monologue on this era of free agency.

The Patriots are great. Swallow it straight, with no chaser.

A few things became obvious when the Patriots won Super Bowl XXXVIII, 32-29 over the Carolina Panthers:

Adam Vinatieri is one of the best clutch athletes New England sports fans have ever seen. We're not just talking about clutch kickers or clutch football players. We're talking athletes, regardless of the sport and regardless of the decade.

Vinatieri and his teammates can start their own drama club.

Tom Brady has played in two Super Bowls, has led two winning drives in the final 90 seconds, and has to make room for another MVP Cadillac in his Quincy, Mass., garage.

Bill Belichick is the top head coach in the NFL, Scott Pioli is the league's leading personnel man, and Robert Kraft is the most exceptional of Paul Tagliabue's 32 owners.

And, of course, there is this: A team that wins 15 consecutive games has to be considered one of the finest in the history of the league.

"It's us and it's the [undefeated] 1972 Dolphins," Patriots vice chairman Jonathan Kraft said on the floor of Reliant Stadium. He was holding the Lombardi Trophy high above his head when he said it. The trophy had long lost its glitter because it was covered with fingerprints. They were the fingerprints of players, coaches, medical staff, video staff, families, and friends.

That has always been the beauty of this Patriots team. It was brilliantly built, built in such a way that one man cannot disrupt the system. It was built with corny words—spirit and soul and integrity—in mind as well.

"The message," Belichick said, "is that you can do this the right way. You can win with players who are not looking to promote themselves and be selfish. You can win with people who care about the team first."

A lot of coaches say that, but they say it with a trace of fantasy. Belichick and Pioli have seen it happen twice in the past three seasons.

"Here's all you have to know about our team," Belichick said. "We won all those games in a row, and not one person wants to take credit for it. Not one guy. Brady credits the offensive line. The coaches credit the players. Ty [Law] got three interceptions in the AFC Championship game, and he says the pressure from the defensive line made it possible.

"How cool is that?"

Probably as cool as Brady in the fourth quarter last night. The Patriots were leading, 21-16, and were one score from putting the Panthers in a difficult position. On third down at the Carolina 9, Brady threw a pass intended for Christian Fauria. It was intercepted. Carolina turned the turnover into a touchdown that put the Panthers ahead, 22-21.

Then Brady came back with a touchdown to Mike Vrabel—Mike Vrabel!—and watched Kevin Faulk complete the 2-point conversion. Carolina responded with a touchdown, and then Brady again put Vinatieri in position to make a winning kick.

"I don't know if we're the greatest or not," Law said. "But I'll tell you what we'll do. We'll compete against any team."

No, they don't scare you. They don't have steel coming out of their chests as the Steelers of the 1970s did. They didn't win all their games like the Dolphins of '72. Belichick doesn't stalk the sideline like Vince Lombardi, shouting out instructions under the lid of a fedora.

But this team is resourceful. It can win games with defense and it can win by topping 30 points. It can win in nasty conditions, such as the divisional playoff over Tennessee and the AFC East clincher over Miami. It can win ugly games (9-3 over Cleveland, 17-6 over the New York Giants), and it can win games that just may be considered the most thrilling in league history.

The Patriots' victory over the Rams in Super Bowl XXXVI was like that. So was their win over the Panthers. They had plenty to talk about as they partied at the Intercontinental Hotel in Houston after the game. The face of the organization had a collective smile.

The Panthers? It must be said that the losing team was outstanding in this game. The people of the Carolinas should be proud of the tough team that represents them. If the Patriots are truly a dynasty, and it appears that they are, they will know that the Panthers will be a likely Super Bowl dance partner for the next five years.

New England, though, was just a little better and a little tougher. And that's the way the Patri-

ots played all season. They were fallible enough to make every team believe it had a chance. They were skilled and creative enough to handle every tough situation.

Even a source as unlikely as rapper Snoop Dogg found that out before the Patriots' Saturday practice. Snoop, a guest of Willie McGinest's, was taking pictures with several Patriots. When he saw Belichick, Snoop was surprised to hear the coach's first words.

"Hey," Belichick said. "Gin and juice, right?"

That's a reference to one of the rapper's songs. Who knew Belichick was familiar with it? Then again, who knew that all of New England would be presented with a team like this?

BIG CATCH
Deion Branch led the Patriots with 10 receptions for 143 yards, including this one to set up a score.

SECRET WEAPON Mike Vrabel, usually a linebacker, came in at tight end and caught the tying touchdown pass.

THE HERO

The sure thing

by JACKIE MAC MULLAN

THERE ARE VERY FEW THINGS IN LIFE THAT Patriots linebacker Mike Vrabel is absolutely, positively certain about.

Kicker Adam Vinatieri is one of them.

"I was sure he'd make it," said Vrabel, rubbing his son Tyler's head in the afterglow of his team's second Super Bowl victory in three years. "Adam is like Deion Sanders. If he ever messes up, you just know he's going to make sure he'll get the next one.

"It's just unbelievable what he's done. The guy is so deserving of whatever comes his way. He is the best clutch kicker ever, in the history of this league. When he was lining up for that kick, I couldn't even see the goal post, there were so many flashbulbs going off. I would have needed a visor to kick it."

Vinatieri won Super Bowl XXXVIII for the Patriots in the final seconds without wearing anything on his head. He did, however, put on longer spikes at halftime, after a recently sprayed field proved to be a little slicker than he'd like. He would never use that as an excuse for the unthinkable happening in the opening drive. The Patriots got into the habit of scoring the very first time they had the ball, and it appeared they would do the same against a stingy Carolina defense.

Quarterback Tom Brady coaxed his offensive unit down to the 18-yard line, and then it was the kicker's turn. All Vinatieri had to do was line up and boot a 31-yard field goal, which is about as routine for him as lacing up his spikes. But as soon as he kicked it, he knew. Wide right.

"I don't know," mused Vinatieri. "That first one, probably I was a little excited. I probably was a little too fast."

He had always been automatic, particularly during that magical Super Bowl season two years ago, when he kicked five game-winning field goals. The most famous play of his marvelous career—the kick in the snow to eliminate the Oakland Raiders—vaulted him to stardom. It didn't hurt, of course, that when Super Bowl XXXVI ticked down to the final seconds, he lined up and calmly knocked a 48-yard field goal through the uprights to upend the heavily favored St. Louis Rams.

And, so, we got used to expecting him to be perfect—or nearly so. Last year, when the team collectively experienced a Super letdown, Vinatieri was better than ever, successful on 90 percent (27 of 30) of his kicks. It was the highest percentage in the NFL, and as the Patriots staff looked to the future, it never occurred to them to worry about their kicker.

But this season was a trying one for Vinatieri. He struggled with back problems he wasn't supposed to talk about. He struggled with a merry-go-round of snappers and holders, something he wasn't supposed to talk about either. He is a team player, an eternal optimist, and he never—ever—let on to the hordes of media that tromped past his locker how frustrated he was at times. He converted only 25 of 34 field goals in the regular season. He—horrors!—actually missed an extra point.

He was able to wipe the numbers clean each week because he lives by the kicker's mentality: whatever just happened, forget it.

"You don't ever want to ever think about the last kick, good or bad," Vinatieri said. "The only

one you should ever care about is the one in front of you."

So fine. Forget about missing that 31-yarder in the first quarter last night. Forget about the 36-yard attempt that was blocked by Carolina's Shane Burton with six minutes left until halftime.

But wait a minute. Deion Sanders would never forget that. He'd dwell on them until he got himself good and ticked off, and marched back on the field to right his wrongs. He would seep in his own failure until he left himself no choice but to succeed the next time out.

"Well, OK, yeah," Vinatieri acknowledged. "I'm as competitive as anybody. It would be like a receiver dropping the ball, and making sure he got the next one, or a defender blowing a coverage, and making a play the next time. I'm just glad my teammates have that kind of confidence in me."

The kicker has a tricky role on a football team. He does a lot of waiting around, often feeling, as Vinatieri has confessed in the past, a bit disconnected from the team. But when your time comes, you become the most important player on the field. It is a responsibility that Vinatieri has never feared, only craved.

And so he waited, and hoped for another chance. When Carolina quarterback Jake Delhomme's 85-yard bomb to Muhsin Muhammad gave the Panthers a 22-21 lead with 6:53 left, Vinatieri began preparing for a role in the responding drive. That was not necessary when Tom Brady found Vrabel in the end zone. But there was Delhomme again, connecting with veteran Ricky Proehl, and the score was tied, 29-29.

Vinatieri looked up at the scoreboard, and smiled. There was 1:08 left on the clock.

"Even if you ever give us any time, look out," he said.

His quarterback did what he does best: he managed the team down the field. Brady got the ball to the 23-yard line, leaving Vinatieri eight seconds and 41 yards to win it. As he ran onto the field, he surveyed Reliant Stadium, filled with 71,525 screaming fans, and he felt . . . nothing.

Nothing but calm.

"I had no doubt," said linebacker Tedy Bruschi. "I've seen him make kick after kick after kick after kick. How could anyone doubt him?"

As the ball sailed through the uprights, and Vinatieri was mobbed by his teammates (again), poised to be the Super Bowl hero (again), all the misses of a long, long season went poof, like the flashbulbs exploding around him.

He is the best clutch kicker in the business. Try and tell his teammates differently.

"It never gets old," said Vinatieri, when asked how he felt. "It never gets old."

Two Super Bowls. Two winning kicks. That's something no kicker should ever forget.

YEAH!
Adam Vinatieri
has a moment
alone to savor
his winning
field goal.

THE MVP

Mr. Cool

by KEVIN PAUL DUPONT

IT WASN'T AS IF A TATTERED SCRIPT FELL FROM the Reliant Stadium roof, a remnant from New Orleans two Super Bowls ago. But as the final moments played out, Carolina receiver Ricky Proehl felt as if he had seen it all before, the ending playing "Brady going down the field," said Proehl, who two years ago was a member of the St. Louis Rams club that was stunned by New England in the Super Bowl. "The same thing . . . and Vinatieri kicked the field goal. When it was over, I had the sick feeling again."

Cool, calm, and seemingly inflappable, Brady further burnished his image as a clutch postseason performer, connecting on 32 of 48 passes, good for 354 yards and three touchdowns, and pacing the Patriots to a come-from-behind 32-29 Super Bowl victory over the defensively-tenacious Panthers.

The 26-year-old Brady, with only 68 seconds remaining in regulation, once again marched his squad downfield. Over the next 59 seconds, the Patriots chewed up 37 yards in six plays, bringing the ball to the Carolina 23. Over on the sideline, Proehl's stomach was beginning to flip.

"When we need 'em, they cash in," said Deion Branch, reflecting on whether Brady or Vinatieri was the calmest under pressure. "Both of 'em [are the same]. The coaches always say, 'When your number's called, you've got to cash in.'"

Brady further cashed in after the win when he was named the MVP, winning a Cadillac XLR. He also was named the MVP two years ago.

Branch and Brady tried to connect to open the winning drive, but the result was the last of Brady's 16 incompletions. Then came a 13-yard pass to Troy Brown, followed by another to Brown for 20 more, which was nullified for offensive pass interference. Brown redeemed himself with a 13-yard catch on the next snap. The next two plays had Brady first hitting Daniel Graham for 4 more yards, and then a 17-yard hookup wiith Branch. The ball was at the Carolina 23, and Vinatieri was on his way in from the sideline.

"I was just trying to get it a little closer there to shorten the field goal," said Branch. "They had a short coverage there, because they figured out what we were doing. My thought there is, if I can score, I try to score, but I just want to get as close for Adam as I can."

Brady, his helmet off, watched from the sideline as Vinatieri ripped through the ball with his right foot. It couldn't have been more than 10 feet into flight when Vinatieri, who earlier missed a chip shot and had another attempt blocked, raised a clenched right fist. He knew where it was going, and he knew the Patriots were going home winners.

"Adam drilled it right down the middle to win it," said a beaming Brady, sounding more California mellow than East Coast jubilant at the postgame podium. "What a game. What a game. Fitting for a Super Bowl, I guess."

The Patriots had not trailed since last being in Houston Nov. 23. But neither Brady nor anyone else on the New England sideline so much as flinched under the pressure.

"We've been down before," he said. "We just don't lose composure."

If not for the winning drive, Brady risked his signature moment of the night being his pass, intended for Christian Fauria with 7:48 remaining in the fourth, that Reggie Howard picked off in the end zone and ran back to the 10. Four plays later, Jake Delhomme threw an 85-yard touchdown pass to Muhsin Muhammad, ultimately lifting the Panthers to the 22-21 lead.

Flustered? Who, Brady?

"That's what happens in the Super Bowl, you know?" said Brady. "They make great plays, too."

There is a confidence in the Patriots, said Brady, in which they believe they can "win anything."

"But to win this, the way we did it," he added. "It's just unbelievable the way we did it." Two Super Bowls. A pair of victories. Matching MVPs. The inevitable comparisons to former 49ers great Joe Montana.

"I said all week, he's the benchmark for quarterbacks in the league," said Brady, gingerly sidestepping undesired pressure one last time. "This is only my fourth year, and in no way am I close to that. Hopefully one day I'm on that level, but not yet."

REPEAT
Tom Brady won the Super Bowl's MVP award for a second time.

THE DRIVE

Like clockwork

by JOHN POWERS

THIS TEAM GENUFLECTS TO NOBODY. NOT IF there's still time on the clock and a championship trophy waiting at the other end of the field. The Patriots did not take a knee, did not play for overtime when they shocked the Rams to win their first Super Bowl two years ago. They were not going to take a knee against the Panthers, not with 68 seconds left to them, not with only a few stripes to cover to get Adam Vinatieri within range. And the Carolina Panthers knew it.

"Play to win," said Carolina defensive tackle Brentson Buckner, after Vinatieri's magic right foot had broken the Panthers' hearts. "That's what you do. You play to win. You don't play to go into overtime. They did what they needed to do."

There was less time on this final drive than there was against St. Louis, when quarterback Tom Brady had 1:30 to work with. But there also was less real estate to cover after New England got the ball on its own 40 after Carolina had scored to tie the game at 29.

"We had 1:08 and three timeouts," said offensive coordinator Charlie Weis. "That made the play calls a little easier, especially when [John Kasay's] kickoff went out of bounds. Instead of having to go 40 or 50 yards, we only had to go 30 to where we know Adam has a chance at it."

Problem was, after three plays and 24 seconds, the Patriots had moved only 3 yards, after a questionable offensive pass interference call on receiver Troy Brown brought the ball back to the 43 instead of putting it on the Panthers' 27.

Still, the Carolina front four hadn't been getting to Brady, who was sitting patiently in the shotgun as his underappreciated offensive line held off Julius Peppers and friends all night. Now, he calmly picked the Panthers' secondary apart.

Brady went right back to Brown on first and 20 for 13 yards, threading the ball between linebacker Will Witherspoon and cornerback Terry Cousin. "We were in a zone," said Panthers safety Mike Minter, "and they put the ball right in the perfect spot."

Twenty seconds left now, second and 7 with the ball on the Carolina 44 and Vinatieri warming up his leg on the sideline. Here was Brady throwing again, this time a 4-yarder to tight end Daniel Graham to the 40 a second timeout.

Now came the play, on third and 3, that went for Carolina's throat with 14 seconds left. "It was a combo route with Brown and Deion Branch," Weis said. And it caught the Panthers guessing wrong.

Would Brady look for Brown quickly on the shallow route for the first down and maybe a bit more? Or would he risk a longer throw that would put them within field goal range? "They bit on the shallow route," said Weis, "and Deion was open up top, and Brady hit him the way he always does."

Brady had been outgaming the Panthers for most of the evening. As soon as he saw their coverage, he figured a ball to Branch for 17 yards to the 23 was the bull's-eye call.

"I think we had the perfect play called for that coverage," Brady said. "We were really anticipating what they were going to do and Deion ran a great route. I just laid it up there for him and he made a great catch. And it gave us just enough time to call a timeout, and then Adam to run on the field."

Nine seconds left now, which is an eternity for this team. "If you ever give us any time," mused Vinatieri, "look out." The Panthers called a timeout to ice him, but they were merely crossing their fingers.

Vinatieri had only missed four of his 35 previ-

ous indoor attempts, but all of them had come in-side Reliant Stadium. The first had missed just wide. The second had been blocked by massive defensive tackle Shane Burton.

But the Panthers, who'd seen the film clip of Vinatieri's previous Super Bowl winner a million times, weren't counting on him missing a second time. Not from 41 yards in the middle of the field.

"I wasn't thinking about him missing," said

defensive end Mike Rucker. "I was thinking about us blocking it. But we just weren't able to get that one."

Not even close. Vinatieri drilled the ball right down Main Street and halfway to downtown, and the Patriots had won their second ring in three years.

"It never gets old," Vinatieri declared. "It never, ever gets old."

FOCUS
Tom Brady lines up to hit Deion Branch with the pass to set up the winning field goal.

CELEBRATE
Rodney Harrison, his arm in a sling, takes in his first championship with the Patriots.

COLTS

FOXBOROUGH

24-14

JANUARY 18
2003

32 DEGREES
SNOWING

Crowning moment

by DAN SHAUGHNESSY

FIRST DOWNS	RUSHING YARDS	PASSING YARDS	TURNOVERS
NE 20 | 21 IND	112 | 98	237 | 208	2 | 5

IN THE END, IT WAS MORE CELEBRATION THAN contest, more coronation than competition.

The New England Patriots are going to the Super Bowl for the fourth time in franchise history, the second time in three years: New England vs. the Carolina Panthers in Super Bowl XXXVIII at Reliant Stadium in Houston.

In a final, flurried, fun-filled afternoon at Gillette Stadium, the Patriots won their 14th consecutive game, a 24-14 dismantling of the Indianapolis Colts in the AFC Championship game. There was little artistic about the win, but

SACKS	PENALTIES	TIME OF POSSESSION	RECORD
4|0	3|4	32:14|27:46	16-2|14-5

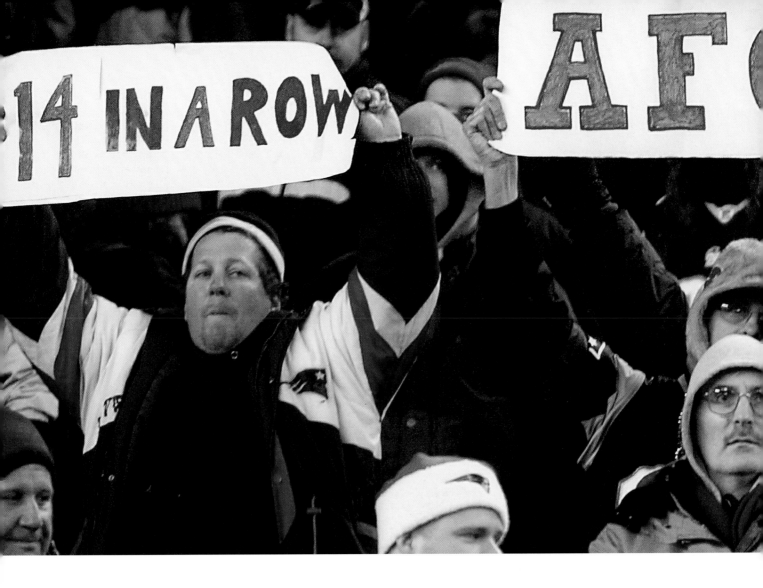

the Patriots again demonstrated that theirs is the best defense in the NFL.

"To win 14 in a row is unbelievable," said everblessed quarterback Tom Brady. "Who does that? Nobody does that. Still, the goal really hasn't been achieved if we don't get 15. Then it's all for naught . . . But I'm proud to be quarterback of a team that's going to the Super Bowl two times in three years."

Brady and the Patriots won the 2002 Super Bowl in New Orleans against the Rams, one of the epic upsets in football history. This time, New England will be favored. Bill Belichick's 16-2 team is the best team in franchise history, and by closing with 15 straight wins could go down as one of the best in the annals of the NFL.

Just look at what happened. Peyton Manning and Co. came to Foxborough on the heels of two of the greatest offensive performances in playoff lore, then limped out of Gillette with an acute case of Mad Colt Disease. Indianapolis turned the ball over five times and bumbled a punt attempt (errant snap) into a safety. The previously indomitable Manning was intercepted four times — thrice by Ty Law — completed fewer than half of his passes, and didn't get his

team on the scoreboard until the third quarter.

"The real thrill was being able to do it in front of our fans," said Patriots owner, Bob Kraft – the most popular and successful Boston pro sports owner since Walter Brown steered the Bill Russell Celtics. "The fans are the 12th man that helped us go 12-0 [including the exhibition season] at home."

Upon accepting the Lamar Hunt trophy, signifying AFC supremacy, Kraft told the lingering 68,000, "We want you all down there in Houston and let's bring that trophy back."

With so many veterans of Super Bowl XXXVI still around, the Patriots did not go overboard in celebration (remember the Red Sox and that ridiculous wild-card clincher?). They donned AFC champion hats and T-shirts, but there were no champagne baths in the winner's locker room.

"It's just another game for us in a way," said All-Pro defensive end Richard Seymour. "It's a step on the way to our ultimate goal."

They will miss the zany masses who filled the Razor 12 times. In the second year of the stadium's existence, the Patriots' crib became the toughest place to win. Fans braved traffic, heat,

rain, snow, 3-foot drifts, parking nightmares, and wind chill temperatures of 10-below zero. None of it mattered. They came early, stayed late, and shook down the thunder every time the PA played Gary Glitter's Rock 'n' Roll Part 2. Sixty-eight thousand 12th men and women. Not bad.

The final home game could not have started in better fashion for New England. With friendly flakes falling, the Patriots took the opening kiczkoff and marched 65 yards in 13 plays, scoring on a 7-yard touchdown pass from Brady to David Givens. The Patriots led, 7-0, and just as important, almost half of the first quarter was already over.

Manning moved the Colts to the New England 7-yard line, then was intercepted in the end zone by Rodney Harrison. It was a terrible throw. It was also Manning's first interception of the 2004 playoffs. He had eight touchdown passes and no picks in the indomitable victories over Denver and Kansas City.

A 31-yard Adam Vinatieri field goal made it 10-0 early in the second, Then came the first and most spectacular of Law's three interceptions. Think Carl Yastrzemski, April of '67, ninth inning, grabbing Tom Tresh's liner to

deep left in Billy Rohr's no-hit bid. A 25-yard field goal followed and it was 13-0. At that point, the Colts' only two possessions had both ended with interceptions.

Indy's next offensive series resulted in the Colts lining up for their first punt of the playoffs. Colt long snapper Justin Snow hiked the ball over Hunter Smith's head. The rusty punter gave chase and booted the ball across the opposite goal line. The result of the chaos was a Patriot saftey and a 15-0 lead.

The Colts gave the Patriots a couple of scares in the second half, but any time things got tight, the New England defense did the job.

So like the Kennedys in Massachusestts, the Patriots went undeated in their home state. And now there's only one game left. Indoors – without all the trappings of home.

"I don't think we're going to have to worry about the snow or 20-below wind chills or anything like that," said Vinatieri, the undisputed king of bad-weather kickers.

No more snow. No more cold. No more Gillette.

Just the Super Bowl. The final crowning for the best football team New England ever has known.

BOB KRAFT "The fans are the 12th man that help us go 12-0 at home."

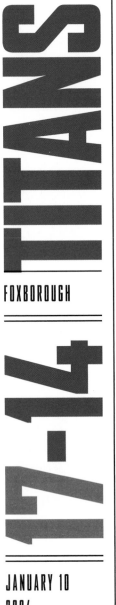

TITANS

FOXBOROUGH

17-14

JANUARY 10
2004

4 DEGREES
WINDY

Shivering heights

by MICHAEL SMITH

GIVE HIM CREDIT. HE CALLED IT. BILL Belichick predicted that the AFC divisional play-off game at Gillette Stadium against the Tennessee Titans would be the Patriots' toughest game of the season. It sounded like a cliche when he said it. But Belichick couldn't have been more accurate.

Playing in the coldest game in franchise history (4 degrees, minus-10 windchill at kickoff), the top-seeded Patriots held on for a 17-14 win over the wild-card Titans. Adam Vinatieri, who had missed a 44-yard field goal in the first quarter, gave New England its 13th straight win with a 46-yarder with 4 minutes 6 seconds to play.

The Titans made it interesting on their last possession, driving 36 yards to New England's 40 before self-destructing after the two-minute warning. First, Tennessee was penalized 10 yards for intentional grounding by Steve Mc-Nair. Guard Benji Olson's holding penalty pushed the Titans back another 10 yards and put them in a third-and-22 situation.

McNair threw 10 yards to Drew Bennett on third down. On fourth and 12 from New England's 43, Rodney Harrison's blitz forced McNair to throw up a jump ball to Bennett, who bobbled it and had it knocked away by Asante Samuel.

"It was everything we expected of this game," Belichick said. "All their key players played well. We were fortunate to make more plays than Tennessee did."

"It was one of the more intense games I've played in," Harrison said.

The Patriots gained 297 yards to the Titans' 284. McNair played like a co-MVP, completing 18 of 26 passes for 210 yards. But, as it has all season, New England's defense stiffened when it had to. "It was our season," Harrison said. "We had let them go downfield, and enough was enough. We challenged them. We stepped up and said if they're going to beat us, they're going to beat us. You can't let him sit back there and

sling the ball. We decided to try something different and give him a different look."

After the game the Patriots did not have the look of a team that was a win away from the Super Bowl. "We're not jumping for joy in here," Tedy Bruschi said. "We know what we want to do. We're just one step closer."

"We're not looking at the Super Bowl. We're looking at one game at a time," said Harrison, repeating what has become a familiar refrain. "You don't see guys jumping around. We're focused."

Titans guard Zach Piller was not impressed, even after the Patriots had beaten the Titans for a second time this season. "Everyone was talking about their defense," Piller said. "I thought it sucked. It'd be a shock to me if they were holding the trophy at the end of all of this. . . . I will not leave this stadium thinking we got beat by a better team. I think that that team is not a very good team and it sickens me that we lost to them. It just wasn't our day."

The Titans took their first possession of the second half and marched 70 yards in 11 plays, tying the game on Steve McNair's 11-yard collaboration with Derrick Mason. The drive took 7:47 and included a 30-yard completion from McNair to Tyrone Calico. On the touchdown, Mason took McNair's short pass, slipped the attempted tackle of Asante Samuel, and leaped over Tyrone Poole and the pylon.

New England hadn't committed any major errors until tight end Daniel Graham fumbled (Kevin Carter forced it) and the Titans' Carlos Hall recovered near midfield. But the Patriots' defense didn't budge, forcing Tennessee into a three and out. Credit Willie McGinest for the stop; he blew up an attempted screen to Frank Wycheck, tackling the tight end for a 10-yard loss on first down.

That set the stage for the fourth quarter and more heroics from Vinatieri and the defense.

FIRST DOWNS		RUSHING YARDS	PASSING YARDS	TURNOVERS
NE 18	16 TEN	96 84	201 200	1 1

ON TARGET
From the hold of Ken Walter, Adam Vinatieri's 46-yard field goal is true to beat the Titans in the fourth quarter.

SACKS	PENALTIES	TIME OF POSSESSION	RECORD
4 0	2 9	28:02 31:58	15-2 13-5

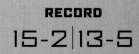

☆ ☆ ☆ ☆ ☆ ☆ ☆ ☆ ☆ ☆ ☆ ☆ ☆

A season of focus

by JOHN POWERS

January is the month of both anticipation and reflection, named after the two-faced Roman god who looked both forward and backward. If Janus played for the Patriots, though, he'd be wearing blinkers. In Bill Belichick's myopic universe, December never happened and February is a century away.

"Everybody is 0-0 now," Belichick said, as soon as the regular season ended. "We all know what it is. Lose, and you are out. Win, and you keep going. That is it.

New England's achievements in the regular season were impressive and undeniable—a franchise-record 14 victories, the last 12 in a row. A perfect home record. The best defense in club history.

"It doesn't matter how you got here," said Belichick. "Whether you won them in a row, didn't win them in a row, however it happened."

The Patriots got here by living exclusively in the moment, by ignoring previous and future Sundays, by using the players available to them, by accepting—and adjusting to—conditions as they found them, and by expecting to win every game by whatever means necessary.

RUSHING OFFENSE	PASSING OFFENSE	SCORING OFFENSE	TURNOVER RATIO
100.4 (27th)	214.5 (9th)	348 (12th)	+17 (2d)

TOM TERRIFIC
Quarterback Tom Brady made all the plays down the stretch for the streaking Patriots.

RUSHING DEFENSE	PASSING DEFENSE	SCORING DEFENSE	PENALTIES
89.6 (4th)	202 (15th)	238 (1st)	111 (22st)

It's not like we're Pavlov's dogs or anything," mused linebacker Ted Johnson. "But we're conditioned to prepare a certain way."

That was how Belichick's charges smacked down Philadelphia after losing to Buffalo in the worst opening-game defeat in franchise history, how they knocked off Tennessee after losing to Washington.

That was how the Patriots smothered the Giants with nine starters missing, how they ended the Miami jinx, how they outfoxed Denver, outlasted Houston, and outpointed Indianapolis. "New England just outcoached, outpersonneled, and outplayed everybody," conceded Tom Donahoe, Buffalo's president and general manager.

Nobody was saying that after the Bills destroyed New England, 31-0, in Game 1, just days after star safety Lawyer Milloy went from teammate to opponent. The Patriots were pathetic on defense in their debut, punchless on offense. "This wasn't us today," acknowledged linebacker Mike Vrabel.

Were they distracted by the Milloy changeover? Poorly prepared? Overrated? Did they hate their coach, as ESPN commentator Tom Jackson later opined? "There is a lot of football left to be played," observed Belichick, who said on that Sunday that he wasn't looking past Monday. "It is short-term, and it is day-by-day."

Game 2 would be against a different team in a different place with a different game plan. The Eagles eventually won their division, but that day they were missing half of their secondary.

So quarterback Tom Brady threw three play-action touchdown passes, two to tight end Christian Fauria, the defense harassed Donovan McNabb into a brutal performance (18 of 46 for 186 yards with no touchdowns, eight sacks, and two interceptions, one for a touchdown by Tedy Bruschi) and New England left the field a 31-10 victor.

It's already forgotten

One Sunday had nothing to do with the next. That was the Belichick credo. What he hated most about his job, he would say, was returning to the locker room at 4 o'clock after a loss, a week's preparation gone for naught. But at 4:01, the next Sunday began, with another chance for victory.

"Every game we've played since I've been here, we felt like we were going to win," Belichick said. "We obviously didn't win all of them, but that's how we felt going in."

Which is why the 20-17 loss at Washington in Game 4—the last defeat of the regular season—rankled. The squad was missing five offensive and four defensive starters that day, and Brady's throwing shoulder and elbow were hurting. But the players still expected to prevail.

"We should have won the game," said Bruschi, after the Patriots had climbed out of a 20-3 hole and tried a fourth-down pass in the final minute instead of going for a tying field goal. "To say it was a moral victory, you're asking me to settle, and I won't. I won't settle for any loss."

Even if nearly half of the lineup was on crutches. Football is a smashmouth sport and broken bones and ripped ligaments are routine and always will be. "The game is going to move on," said safety Rodney Harrison.

And the rules still call for 11 men on the field, whether or not they'd expected to be there. "We're a 53-man roster," said guard Joe Andruzzi. "Nobody's here to collect a backup-role check. If someone goes down, you have to be able to step up."

With its regulars missing 103 games with injuries, New England plugged in 42 different starters and used the same lineup for consecutive games only once. The defense, which lost one linebacker (Rosevelt Colvin) for the season, another (Johnson) for eight games, and nose tackle Ted Washington for six more, switched from a 3-4 scheme to a 4-3, then back again five times.

"Right now, we're just willing ourselves," said cornerback Tyrone Poole, after the Patriots had survived a wet and grimy wrangle with the Giants in Game 6.

They still were minus nine starters. They managed just 29 yards in the first half and eight pass completions for the game. They converted just 1 of 11 third downs and committed 10 penalties. Yet they still won, 17-6, because the defense made four interceptions and Matt Chatham returned a fumble 38 yards for a touchdown. "Man, that was a great win for our football team," declared Belichick.

The greatest, though, came the following week at Miami, where New England had never won a game in September or October (as in 0-13). "We've got to get those guys," vowed guard Damien Woody. "They beat the crap out of us. It's been ugly games down there ever since I came here."

With two minutes left in regulation and Dolphins kicker Olindo Mare setting up for a 35-yard field goal, the Patriots appeared squelched again. Mare had only had two of 201 career attempts blocked. "What are the chances?" asked defensive lineman Richard Seymour, after he'd batted the ball away to force overtime.

Then, after losing the coin toss, New England shrewdly chose to defend the west end of Pro Player Stadium, where the baseball infield was, to force Mare to kick on dirt.

After Mare missed right, Brady promptly lofted an 82-yard touchdown pass to Troy Brown for the 19-13 victory that made both the Patriots and their fans believe that anything was possible. "If you look back," said center Dan Koppen, "that was the turning point for this team."

The starters would vary, the game plans change, but week after week, there was a victory. Almost all of them were close—11 straight times, New England won by two touchdowns or less, an NFL record. And most went down to the final minutes. "We're just going to play it out and when 60 minutes is up, we'll see how it ends," said Woody, after his mates had subdued Cleveland, 9-3. "See who's the last one standing."

The triumphs often were grinding and graceless, like the 12-0 throttlings of Dallas and Miami. But Belichick didn't care about style points, as long as the day ended in a W. "It's hard to win in this league," he said. "However you can win, you better be happy about it."

Even if it meant clanging a snap off the goal post for an intentional safety, as Lonie Paxton did in Denver with the Patriots trailing by a point with less than three minutes to play and backed up against their end zone.

After Ken Walter's free kick chased the Broncos back to their 15 and the defense forced them three-and-out, Brady threw an 18-yard touchdown pass to David Givens with 30 seconds left for a 30-26 victory. "It was a horrible knife in the guts for Denver," Hunter S. Thompson observed on ESPN.com.

It was all about execution under pressure, Belichick said. The Patriots beat Houston in overtime by stopping the Texans three times, then kicking a field goal with 41 seconds to play. Then, after squandering a three-touchdown lead in the second half, they slammed the door on the Colts by stacking them up three times at the 1-yard-line with less than 25 seconds to play.

"To be the best, you've got to stop the best," said linebacker Willie McGinest, after he'd lassoed Edgerrin James on fourth down. "And we did that."

Their defense (ranked seventh) and offense (17th) weren't at the top of the NFL statistical page and they only had two players (Seymour and cornerback Ty Law) chosen for the Pro Bowl.

But the Patriots won those 14 games by using their entire roster and by focusing on the statistics that produce victories—points allowed (a league-low 14.9, a franchise record), a turnover differential of plus-17 (another franchise record), an NFL-high six defensive touchdowns, and red-zone scoring (42 of 50, 22 of them touchdowns).

Mostly, though, they won them by recognizing that each victory was merely a down payment on something more important. "We're not going to sit here and have a parade and celebrate because we won five games," said Belichick, after his squad had ended its tropical hex at Miami. "We just haven't done anything yet."

BILLS

31-0

ORCHARD PARK,
NEW YORK

SEPTEMBER 7
2003

72 DEGREES
SUNNY

Haunted by an old friend

by NICK CAFARDO

IT WAS AS IF THE BILLS WERE THE PATRIOTS AND the Patriots were the Bills. It was as if Tom Brady was Drew Bledsoe, and vice versa. It was Buffalo coach Gregg Williams being asked whether he had gotten into Brady's head, with nobody wondering if the Patriots' Bill Belichick got into Bledsoe's head, as is often the case.

After 2002's two lopsided Patriots wins, one might have expected a downtrodden Buffalo team and an upbeat New England squad, and a Patriots victory. What happened, a 31-0 Buffalo win, the worst opening day loss in Patriots history, was just the opposite.

Five days after Lawyer Milloy's release from the Patriots over a contract dispute, he was still on the winning side of a game the Bills could not have orchestrated any better. Milloy, who started at strong safety, made five tackles and was credited with an 11-yard sack of Brady. He made a key play by defending a pass in the back of the end zone intended for David Patten, enabling Nate Clements to grab the deflection for an interception.

The last starter introduced, Milloy came out with a new dance that he had especially designed for his new fans. "I don't think the Bills needed Lawyer to get them going," said Patriots guard Mike Compton. "The rest of their guys outplayed us in every phase of the game."

The Patriots were flat from the outset.

If there was one other undeniable fact about the Bills, it was that their revamped defense seems like it may be special. At least it was on this warm day before 73,262 at Ralph Wilson Stadium. To shut out the Patriots, who were last blanked Nov. 8, 1993, 6-0, by the Jets, was over-

FIRST DOWNS	RUSHING YARDS	PASSING YARDS	TURNOVERS
NE 16 | 23 BUF	105 | 104	134 | 215	4 | 2

HELLO, AGAIN
Tom Brady gets reacquainted with—and sacked by—an old friend and former teammate, Bills safety Lawyer Milloy.

SACKS	PENALTIES	TIME OF POSSESSION	RECORD
2 | 2	12 | 10	26:10 | 33:50	0-1 | 1-0

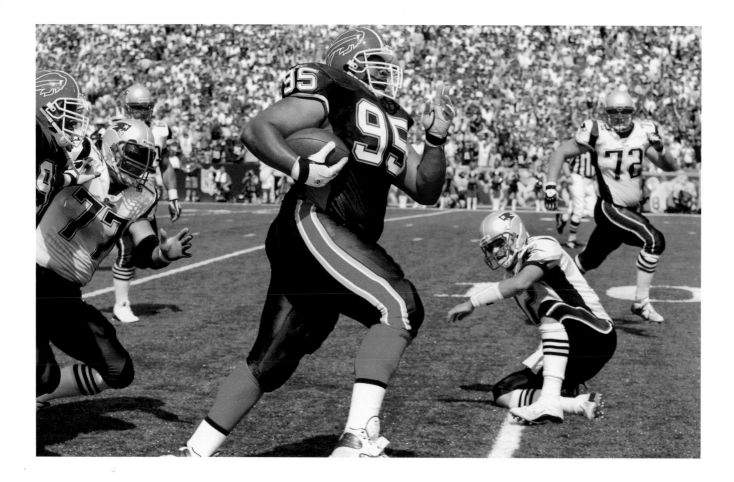

whelming evidence. Newcomers Takeo Spikes and Sam Adams were big differences on a defense that ran over the Patriots, limiting Brady to a 14-for-29 effort for 123 yards and four interceptions, clearly his worst as a Patriot.

"There was nothing good that came out of that game," said Brady. "It's the first time we've faced adversity in six weeks and we've got to rebound. From the opening kickoff to the last play of the game, it was all one-sided."

Adams sealed the game when he picked off Brady with 10:24 remaining in the second quarter. The big man rambled 37 yards down the right sideline, carrying the pigskin like Ricky Williams but doing this "40" in perhaps the slowest time in NFL history. Yet blocks by London Fletcher and Aaron Schobel kept him protected, making it 21-0.

"Our defense," said an ecstatic Bledsoe, "Jeez. They were tremendous out there."

Bledsoe, who was 17 for 28 for 230 yards, with one touchdown and one interception, wasn't bad either. When Bledsoe can play with a lead, not force balls into coverage, and use his running game, it's usually going to be a long day for the opposition. Another ex-Patriot, Sam Gash, opened up good holes as a lead blocker for Travis Henry, who ran 28 times for 86 yards.

The Patriots actually ran the ball well, gaining 105 yards on 21 carries, Kevin Faulk accounting for 62 yards, but many of the runs came when the

Bills were defending a 21-point halftime lead.

The Bills stuffed it right down the Patriots' throats on their first possession, marching 80 yards in nine plays. The Bills converted two third-down plays on the drive (they were 7 for 14 on third down in the game) and Bledsoe connected on a 24-yard pass to Bobby Shaw over Ty Law and Antwan Harris. Law became animated after the play, but denied he was yelling at Harris. Said Harris afterward: "We play a team defense. If they make a play on us, it's a team mistake, not an individual one."

From the Patriots' 20, Law was called for pass interference on Eric Moulds, who had a step on him in the end zone when Law brushed his backside. On first down from the 1, Henry, behind Gash, knocked it in for the 7-0 lead.

With the temperature 72 degrees, Bledsoe kept the Patriots' defense on the field for 15 plays and 9:28 on a 90-yard scoring drive in which nothing went right for the Patriots. Third tight end Fred Baxter committed a defensive holding penalty on a punt, which would have ended the drive at the Patriots' 40. Instead, the Bills kept on moving, and Bledsoe hit wide-open tight end Dave Moore from 7 yards out for 6 more points.

After Adams's play, the Patriots went into the locker room with that huge 21-0 deficit. They have come back from such deficits before, but when they had opportunities to score they didn't take advantage.

☆ ★ ☆ ☆ ☆ ☆ ☆ ☆ ☆ ☆ ☆ ☆ ☆

EAGLES

PHILADELPHIA

31-10

SEPTEMBER 14
2003

82 DEGREES
MOSTLY CLOUDY

A turnaround for Brady

by RON BORGES

AFTER A LONG SEVEN DAYS OF POSTMORTEMS following the worst passing performance of his career in a season-opening 31-0 loss to the Buffalo branch of the Patriots, Tom Brady came back at Lincoln Financial Field as if it was still 2001. He was accurate, not antsy. He was productive, not passive. He was patient, not petulent. He was, in other words, Tom Brady, and the result was not only a 31-10 victory over the Philadelphia Eagles, but an afternoon in which he finished 30 for 44 for 255 passing yards and three touchdowns. His quarterback rating was 105.8, his highest since the Kansas City game in 2002 in which he passed for 410 yards and four touchdowns.

The difference between those two games a year apart was that last season Brady was still The Golden Boy with the Super Bowl MVP under his arm. After last week's terrible defeat, in which he threw four interceptions and finished with an abysmal 22.5 quarterback rating, that award and a lot of other things about his game had been forgotten. Suddenly there were more questions than answers about Brady and the offense he ran and Charlie Weis designed, because it had struggled in the final month last season and seemed to be beginning a new year still on its knees.

Then Brady and Co. arrived in Philadelphia and all was suddenly right with the world again. At least for the moment.

"I didn't sleep much this week," Brady said. "As a quarterback a lot of times you take pride in winning football games. When the team doesn't win and you get defeated, 31-0, and you throw four interceptions, and you get shut out for the first time in how many years, that's tough. At the same time, you need confidence to believe in yourself."

Brady got some of that confidence back in a hurry when he capitalized on two Eagles turnovers in the second quarter and turned them into back-to-back touchdown passes off play-action fakes. Both times those fakes froze the defense for just long enough to allow tight end Christian Fauria to break free in the end zone. Both times Brady found him, as he had so often last season, and those throws made the score 17-7. From that point on, the Eagles were reeling.

When he threw a third score to Deion Branch, also off play-action, midway through the third quarter to make it 24-7, it left Philadelphia quarterback Donovan McNabb in the same position Brady was in a week ago. He was playing behind the eight ball, a position that most often leads to mistakes and more misery. Not to mention some sleepless nights.

"I think we had great field position [because of the forced turnovers]," Brady said. "Our defense created great field position. We scored some points early off those turnovers to take the lead. At the point we went up 17 points, they're running uphill. With your back against the wall you can't use the full gamut of your playbook."

Brady knows well about that because he just lived it. That is how quickly things can change in the NFL based on circumstances and fortunes. One week you are in a hole and cannot get out of it. Seven days later, after a lot of tossing and turning in your bed, you are pushing your opponent into a hole just as deep.

That is life in the NFL, especially for the signal-caller.

"Certainly playing with a lead we took advantage of a lot of different situations," Brady said. "The more times you can possess the ball [the better]. The defense forcing those [six] turnovers, that was huge for us."

Against the Bills, the Patriots' offense had the ball for only three plays in the first quarter and for barely 10 minutes in the first half. Brady threw those four INTs that day, and the Bills capitalized on them.

Against the Eagles it was the opposite, with New England's offense controlling the ball for the first 20 minutes of the game to the Eagles' 10.

FIRST DOWNS	RUSHING YARDS	PASSING YARDS	TURNOVERS
NE 17 | 23 PHI	62 | 99	247 | 169	0 | 6

ON TARGET
Tom Brady gets his 'A' game back and the Patriots' first win in the bank for 2003.

SACKS	PENALTIES	TIME OF POSSESSION	RECORD
7 | 2	8 | 7	36:35 | 23:25	1-1 | 0-2

HIGH ROAD
Tedy Bruschi goes over a blocker to get at Donovan McNabb as the Patriots' defense forced six turnovers and made seven sacks.

HIGH KICK Christian Fauria gets a kick out of making a touchdown catch — one of two he made after play-action fakes by the Patriots.

JETS

23-16

FOXBOROUGH

SEPTEMBER 21
2003

71 DEGREES
SUNNY

Overcoming the pain

by NICK CAFARDO

THE EFFECTS OF MOUNTING INJURIES MAY TAKE their toll down the road, but for the second straight week, the New England Patriots looked at the casts, wraps, and braces square in the eye and laughed. Rosevelt Colvin (hip) out for the season? Ted Johnson (foot) out until Week 12? Mike Compton out with a foot injury? Injuries during the game to Ted Washington (fractured left leg), David Patten (right leg), Mike Vrabel (arm injury, extent unknown), and Ty Law (right ankle sprain)?

It didn't matter.

The JVs stepped in and played just fine as the Patriots improved to 2-1 with a 23-16 win in their Gillette Stadium home opener, a game in which the Patriots turned Jets mistakes into points while the Jets failed to convert on New England's mistakes.

It was nickel back Asante Samuel's 55-yard interception return for a touchdown to open the fourth quarter that ultimately did in the Jets (0-3). Vinny Testaverde, 39, made a terrible mistake and underthrew to Wayne Chrebet, who slipped on his break, allowing Samuel to make the biggest play of his short NFL career, juggling the ball for a moment before running to paydirt.

"Coach made a good call and put me in the right position to make the play," said the rookie corner from Central Florida. "It was a good feeling. It made me feel like I was on Cloud Nine. I was man-to-man on Chrebet and he was shifting and shaking and I waited for him to make his break. I'd never returned one for a touchdown before. Every time I'd get to to the 40 and the 30 and the 20, I'd say to myself, 'You're getting closer, keep going.'"

Oh, he kept going all right, leaving Testaverde, Chrebet, and coach Herm Edwards with a sinking feeling. And yet, the Jets came back and pulled within a touchdown when a breakdown occurred in the New England secondary and Testaverde marched the Jets right down the Patriots' throats, culminating in a 29-yard strike to Chrebet with 12:53 remaining.

But that emptied the Jets' tank.

FIRST DOWNS		RUSHING YARDS	PASSING YARDS	TURNOVERS
NE 19	16 NYJ	147 65	147 264	1 1

HELPING HANDS
Deion Branch lends a hand in the Patriots victory with a pair of receptions.

SACKS	PENALTIES	TIME OF POSSESSION	RECORD
0|5	9|6	32:37|27:23	2-1|0-3

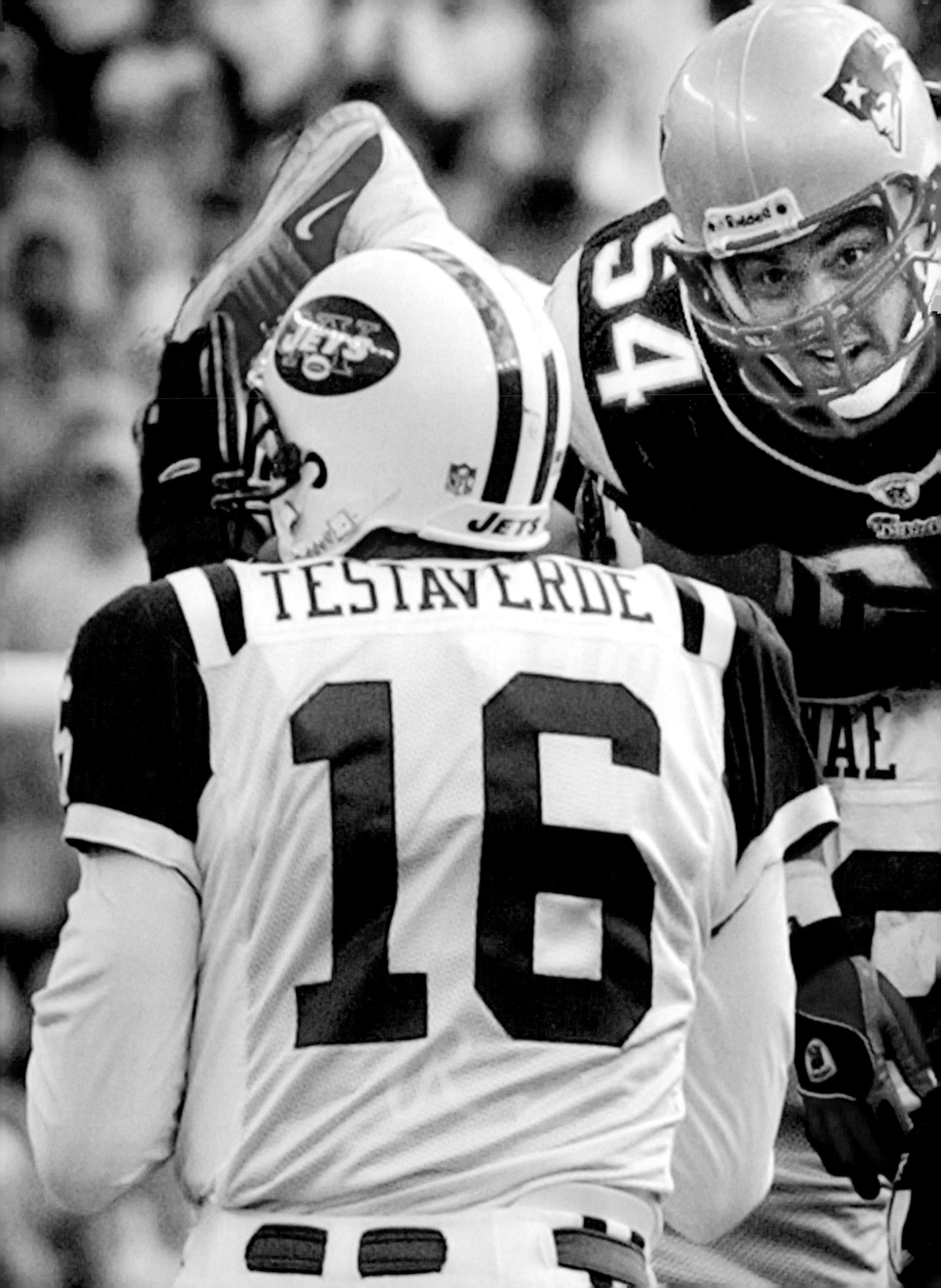
TESTAVERDE
16
54

It was 9-9 (three field goals each by Adam Vinatieri and Doug Brien) when the Patriots marched it 73 yards in seven plays, highlighted by a wide open 28-yard gain on a Tom Brady-to-Christian Fauria connection. On a second-and-10 from the 20, Brady threw toward Troy Brown in the end zone, and he drew an interference call on Ray Mickens, who was subbing for the injured Donnie Abraham. Mickens seemed to have great position, but he failed to turn to the ball. The ball was spotted at the 1, from where Brady, unable to find anyone open, skirted a pass rush and ran it in.

"I looked at my first read and he got caught up," Brady said. "The second guy was on the corner; he got caught up. And I looked back to Christian and he had a double team, so I kind of pumped and then fell into the end zone, it looked like. It wasn't a graceful run."

Style points aside, it was a big drive and a big play. It was the first touchdown of a game that had featured a baseball score. It wasn't entirely out of the realm of possibility that it would end as a low-scoring affair. The Patriots made a concerted effort to run the ball, control the clock, and keep their defense fresh on a warm afternoon when the game-time temperature was 71.

Rushing for 147 yards, led by Kevin Faulk (79) and Antowain Smith (55), the Patriots held nearly a five-minute advantage in time of possession. The Patriots ran 36 times and threw it only 25 times, Brady going 15 for 25 for 181 yards with no touchdowns and five sacks.

The Patriots used a makeshift offensive line, moving Damien Woody to Compton's right guard spot, and switching Joe Andruzzi from right guard to left guard. Matt Light once again did a nice job neutralizing John Abraham, who injured his hamstring later in the game and failed to get a sack.

The Patriots defense, decimated by injuries to Washington (who left the game after the fifth play and was replaced by Rick Lyle), Law, and Vrabel, made good on its promise to pay extra attention to Curtis Martin, who gained 53 yards on 15 carries. The Jets were only able to convert 1 of 13 third downs and were 0 for 2 on fourth down attempts.

The Jets had two opportunities to intercept passes and change the momentum. On the Patriots' only touchdown drive, safety Sam Garnes had the ball thrown to him at the goal line, and while he broke up the pass intended for Daniel Graham, he could have thwarted the drive.

"That's why DBs play DB and that's why they're ex-receivers," said Edwards, who also referred to a pass that slipped between linebacker Sam Cowart's hands in the late stages. Cowart could have given the Jets the ball in Patriots territory. "You can't get those back. That's what I told the guys after the game: You've got to make plays when you have a chance to make plays."

OVER THE TOP Tedy Bruschi takes the high road in an attempt to get into Vinny Testaverde's face.

47

REDSKINS

LANDOVER, MD

20-17

SEPTEMBER 28
2003

65 DEGREES
PARTLY CLOUDY

☆ ★ ★ ☆ ☆ ☆ ☆ ☆ ☆ ☆ ☆ ☆ ☆ ☆

Coming up short

by RON BORGES

FIRST DOWNS	RUSHING YARDS	PASSING YARDS	TURNOVERS
NE 23 15 WAS	106 116	281 134	4 0

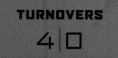

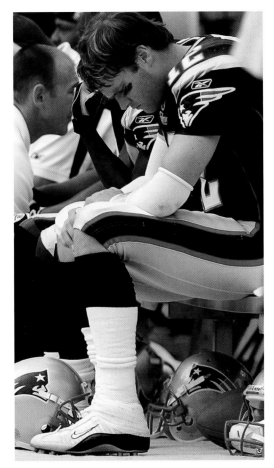

PHYSICALLY, THERE AREN'T MANY THINGS YOU would say Tom Brady does better than the other 31 starting quarterbacks in the NFL. Many of them have stronger arms. Some are more accurate passers. All but a few are more nimble. And there may be a couple—Brett Favre and Steve McNair come to mind—who are as effective a leader.

But none is a more intense competitor. In fact, there may not be a player at any position who takes losing harder than the Patriots' young QB (though if he isn't careful, he'll grow old sooner than he'd like).

That's why Brady needed a few extra moments to collect himself before leaving his locker for the interview room, where he would attempt to explain his throwing three interceptions and, for the first time in memory, failing to deliver in the clutch, leaving New England on the losing end of a 20-17 game against the Washington Redskins. Know this much: Those folding chairs in the visiting locker room at FedEx Field are pretty sturdy; they must be to have supported Brady plus the weight of the world he seemed to be carrying on his slender shoulders long enough for him to memorize the inside of his temporary quarters.

For the first two weeks of the season we've seen Brady shrug off persistent pain in his throwing elbow, but, judging by the look on his face and the way his voice quivered, it took every ounce of his pride to keep from shedding tears following a narrow defeat in which the Patriots faced fourth and 3 from Washington's 38 with 43 seconds to go.

"Everyone's real disappointed," Brady said. "More disappointment than we've had in a while because this is a game we really feel we should have won."

The Patriots trailed, 20-3, when Brady directed a 68-yard drive that ended with a 7-yard touchdown pass to Larry Centers, pulling the Patriots to within 20-17 with 2 minutes 10 seconds left. The Redskins imploded (three false starts) on their next possession, and New England got the ball back at Washington's 45 with 1:39 to go, needing only a first down to get into field-goal range.

Brady threw long and incomplete to Deion Branch on first down, to Centers for 5 yards on second down, and, following Centers's 2-yard run, behind Daniel Graham deep down the middle.

Centers implied after the game that he was open near the first-down marker on New England's final play. "If you complete it, no foul, I'm not disappointed," Center said. "Sometimes you gotta know when to take that shot. I think Tom did a pretty good job for us, we just had some unfortunate things that didn't work out for us."

Brady's judgment has been his hallmark since taking over as the starter two years ago tomorrow, but on an afternoon when he tossed up an ill-advised jump ball to Branch in the end zone—"That was probably the one that [ticked] me off the most," Brady said. "I don't even know if I reached the end zone"—that Ifeanyi Ohalete intercepted, and later tried to squeeze a deep ball to David Givens past Champ Bailey (interception No. 2), one can't help but wonder whether Brady's final decision was an uncharacteristically poor one, as well.

"We had a couple of short receivers," coach

SACKS	PENALTIES	TIME OF POSSESSION	RECORD
1 | 2	8 | 9	33:39 | 26:21	2-2 | 3-1

Bill Belichick said. "It was tight there. The Quarterback probably thought he couldn't get it in. I wouldn't second-guess that one. Troy Brown was short for first-down yardage, but I don't know if it was open."

Graham was for a moment, but the pass appeared behind him, and Ohalete broke it up. "The safety made a good play," Graham said.

Brady made quite a few nice ones himself in the second half, completing 17 of 23 passes for 198 yards and 2 touchdowns, including a pretty 29-yard TD in the third quarter that made it a game again (20-10). But he's known for making them when his team needs them most, and he didn't yesterday.

"A lot of times it comes down to execution," said Brady, dismissing his elbow trouble as a reason for his miscues. "What more can you ask for than what we had? . . . You get the ball with a minute 40 on the 45 and you can't get a first down. That's a pretty bad feeling.

"I'm a better player than that. I don't expect to make plays like that."

ROUGH DAY
Frustration was the operative word for both the New England offense, including Deion Branch (left photo) who couldn't prevent this interception, and the Patriots coach Bill Belichick (above).

51

TITANS

FOXBOROUGH

38-30

OCTOBER 5
2003

53 DEGREES
SUNNY

☆ ★ ☆ ★ ☆ ☆ ☆ ☆ ☆ ☆ ☆ ☆ ☆

A first step

by MICHAEL SMITH

WHILE THE RED SOX WERE "COWBOYING UP" at Fenway Park, the Patriots were "knuckling up" at Gillette Stadium. That was their unofficial rallying cry. That is to say New England wasn't going to back down against one of the league's hardest-hitting teams. The Patriots came looking for a fight with the intention of taking it to Tennessee the way the Titans took it to them in December of 2002.

Truth is, the Patriots took personally all the chatter about how physical Tennessee is. They didn't enjoy having folks come into their 'hood and remind them of how badly they'd been beaten (24-7) in Nashville. It's no wonder, then, the Patriots couldn't wait to catch the Titans on the block.

"They beat the [expletive] out of us last year," guard Damien Woody said. "The only way to put that away was to go out and return the favor."

The Patriots' 38-30 win was not pretty. Entertaining, perhaps, but not pretty. New England's offensive linemen were supposed to get overpowered. Instead, boosted by Woody's return, they handled Tennessee's talented defensive front to the tune of 161 rushing yards. Meanwhile, the Patriots' wounded defense shut down Eddie George and chased Steve McNair as if he had stolen something. And safety Rodney Harrison knocked guys around as though he had been involved in last year's loss.

Don't get it twisted. The Titans didn't just sit there and take it. The game featured seven lead changes. But in the end, after a fast and furious fourth quarter in which the teams combined to score 31 points, the Patriots were the last ones standing, improving to 3-2.

"All week, that's all we heard was how physical they were," said Harrison, who made a team-high 11 tackles, including a third-quarter hit that left Titans tight end Shad Meier with a concussion. "It was up to us to go out there and match their intensity. Going out there, one-on-one, and just knuckling up with those guys. They

have a good team, a very tough team, but our guys played with a lot of heart and a lot of passion."

Perhaps no Patriot displayed more heart than Ty Law. Playing for the second week in a row with a severely sprained right ankle, Law was on the sideline for much of the second half but talked his way back in time to jack McNair's pass intended for Tyrone Calico and limp 65 yards with it for a touchdown that put New England ahead, 38-27, with 1 minute 49 seconds to go.

"I looked at [Law] and I told him, 'I know why you're the best,'" Harrison said. "To hurt his ankle and make a play like that to seal the victory, that was huge. And that just shows what type of player Ty Law is."

No one had a clue what type of runner Mike Cloud would be in his first game since last season. But Cloud, suspended for the first four games of this season for violating the league's substance abuse policy, came off the bench late in the third quarter in relief of Antowain Smith (16 carries, 80 yards, 1 touchdown before leaving with a stinger) and contributed 73 yards on seven attempts, including a 1-yard plunge in the third that put New England ahead, 21-16; a 42-yard jaunt early in the fourth that set up Adam Vinatieri's 48-yard field goal (24-19, Patriots); and a 15-yard touchdown (set up by rookie Bethel Johnson's 71-yard kickoff return) that gave the Patriots the lead for good, 31-27, with a little over three minutes to go.

New England's defense, short no fewer than five regulars, held Tennessee to 70 rushing yards on 27 attempts. Last December at The Coliseum in Nashville, Tennessee ran through, around, and over the Patriots for 238 yards.

"We have heart in here," linebacker Tedy Bruschi said. "We're going to play tough. No matter who's in there, they're going to get the job done. That's what I've been saying the last few weeks. To you guys, I'm sure it's just something where I'm trying to keep the faith. But it's what I believe. We're a tough team."

FIRST DOWNS	RUSHING YARDS	PASSING YARDS	TURNOVERS
NE 21	23 TEN	161	70	193	372	0	1

FEELING GOOD
Ty Law returned to the field with a limp just in time to return this interception for a touchdown.

SACKS	PENALTIES	TIME OF POSSESSION	RECORD
2│3	9│8	28:05│31:55	3-2│3-2

UP IN ARMS
Ty Law's touchdown got the
Gillette Stadium crowd on its
feet and the Patriots' offense,
including Tom Brady and David
Patten, fired up.

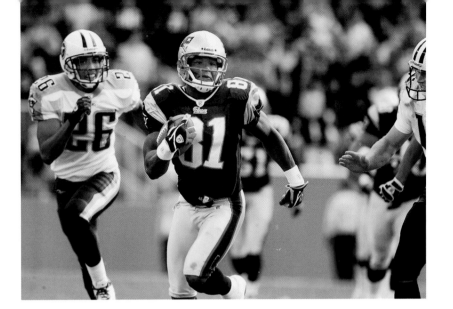

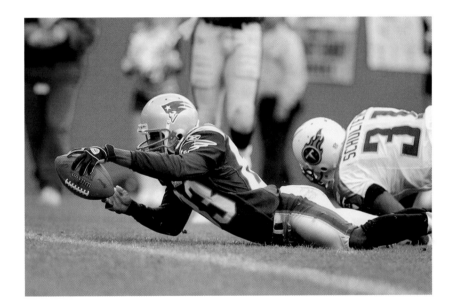

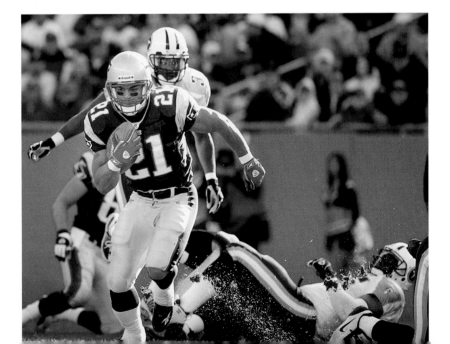

GIANTS

17-6

FOXBOROUGH

OCTOBER 12
2003

55 DEGREES
RAIN

☆ ★ ★ ☆ ★ ★ ☆ ☆ ☆ ☆ ☆ ☆ ☆ ☆ ☆ ☆

True grit

by MICHAEL SMITH

THIS WAS MORE LIKE IT. THOSE SHOOTOUTS, LIKE the one they survived with Tennessee are OK once in a while, but that isn't Patriots football. Too, you know, pretty.

Their brand of ball is gritty. Grimy. Not attractive. Just effective. When they aren't a pleasure to watch, as the Giants learned on a muddy, rainy afternoon at Gillette Stadium, the Patriots can be a pain to play. New England won, 17-6. Had the score been 170-6, it still would have been anatomically impos-

FIRST DOWNS		RUSHING YARDS	PASSING YARDS	TURNOVERS
NE 12	26 NYG	129 75	91 306	0 5

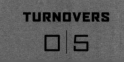

sible for Bill Belichick to wear a wider grin.

"Man, that was a great win for our football team," the Patriots coach said.

The Patriots didn't play great football. Offensively they didn't even play good football. But they played Patriots football. And that was good enough.

The defense forced five turnovers, including four Kerry Collins interceptions (two by Rodney Harrison) and a Tiki Barber fumble (forced by Tyrone Poole) that Matt Chatham returned 38 yards for a touchdown on the Giants' third play from scrimmage. The Giants had the ball for more than 10 more minutes, but the Patriots turned them away twice inside the 20-yard line and five other times inside New England's 30.

The Patriots converted just one of 11 third downs. But that one was a big one—a 21-yard completion from Tom Brady to David Givens on third-and-16 from the Patriots' 9 that kept alive

SACKS	PENALTIES	TIME OF POSSESSION	RECORD
2 | 2	10 | 8	24:47 | 35:13	4-2 | 2-3

their only touchdown drive. They had another solid game on the ground, gaining 129 yards on 31 attempts (4.2-yard average).

So no, it won't go down as one of the season's more memorable games, but this one fits in the only place that will matter come winter: the win column.

"It was just a grind-it-out type game," guard Damien Woody said. "We're not the type of team that puts up 30 or 40 points every week. We're the type of team that grinds it out. We play good, solid defense and complementary offense. A lot of our wins are going to look like this."

"Right now we're just willing ourselves," Poole said.

The Patriots were killing themselves in the first half . They went three and out on five straight possessions and moved the ball 29 yards in 21 plays. Brady went 1 for 10. They managed one first down and committed six penalties. "That was not what we were looking for," Brady said.

Still they led, 7-3, at the break thanks to three New York turnovers and two missed field goals by Brett Conway. They would have had more had they capitalized on Poole's interception of a Collins pass that was deflected by Richard Seymour on the first play from scrimmage. Adam Vinatieri missed a 42-yard field goal. (His fourth

miss in his last six attempts. Worried yet?) "The defense was fantastic," receiver Troy Brown said. "They kept us around until we had a chance to get something going."

The Patriots finally got going because at halftime, out went the game plan. Offensive coordinator Charlie Weis discarded the plan designed to exploit New York's aggressiveness the way Miami had a week earlier in favor of the basics: counters and draws out of three-receiver sets against the Giants' nickel package, and short, safe passes.

The Patriots put together two scoring drives in the third quarter, a nine-play, 63-yard journey that ended with Adam Vinatieri's 28-yard field goal and a 10-play, 85-yard march to Cloud's 1-yard touchdown run. Kevin Faulk stepped in for Cloud and rushed for 85 yards on 13 carries in the second half.

"We tried to block better and eliminate plays," Belichick explained. "Charlie told the team, 'We're not going to run any new plays. Some of the runs we were going to run in this game we're going to forget about it. We're just going to run the stuff that we know and let's stop screwing up.'"

Belichick's bunch is in a position few could have imagined after a bumpy start. They've been steady in some areas, spectacular in none. In other words, they've played Patriots football.

GAME 7

DOLPHINS

MIAMI

19-13

NE | MIA

OCTOBER 19
2003

84 DEGREES
SUNNY

☆ ★ ★ ☆ ★ ★ ★ ☆ ☆ ☆ ☆ ☆ ☆ ☆

Swoon over Miami

by MICHAEL SMITH

SOONER OR LATER, THE HEX, THE CURSE, OR whatever it was had to end.

The streak had to end. And, unfortunately, a quality football game had to end. What a way to end them all.

Tom Brady threw an 82-yard touchdown pass to Troy Brown 9 minutes and 15 seconds into overtime at Pro Player Stadium to give the Patriots a thrilling 19-13 win—New England's first in 14 visits to Miami in September or October—only after Richard Seymour blocked Olindo Mare's attempt at a go-ahead field goal with two minutes remaining in regulation, Mare (the second-most-accurate kicker in league history) missed a 35-yarder in overtime wide right, Brady recovered his own fumble at New England's 40, and Tyrone Poole intercepted Jay Fiedler on Miami's second possession of the extra session.

"It was almost like they were trying to give it to us," Brown said. "It was a matter of time before we took advantage of it."

Guess it was just time. Thirty-seven years was enough. Sixty-nine minutes was enough. The Patriots definitely had had enough of being punked in Miami.

"It was good to get that monkey off our back, coming down here to Miami and losing for I don't know how many years in a row [five]," Brown said after his walk-off touchdown vaulted New England into first place in the AFC East by a half-game over the Dolphins. "It feels good just to come down here and get a win. It was one of those things hanging over our heads. We've been in a couple of those situations. The Jet thing, coming to New England and beating us up for four or five years [five, actually]. Coming down here and losing for I don't know how

FIRST DOWNS	RUSHING YARDS	PASSING YARDS	TURNOVERS
NE 16	20 MIA	59	97	273	229	2	3

FINISHING TOUCH
Troy Brown is on his way to scoring the game-winning touchdown in overtime.

many years in a row in September. Another one of those things to get off your back. Hopefully, next year you guys won't hang it over our heads."

Can't. They've got another streak going. The Patriots have beaten the Dolphins in overtime the last two times they've met. New England overcame a 24-13 deficit with five minutes left in last season's finale to win, 27-24, and keep the Dolphins out of the playoffs. As they did last December, the Dolphins had several opportunities to put the Patriots away. They didn't. Or, worse for their annually failed Super Bowl aspirations, they couldn't.

Miami's Jason Taylor beat Matt Light inside, but Damien Woody was there to back Light up. Brady, having play-faked and pump-faked right, drifted left and—sore elbow, sore shoulder, and all—heaved a deep pass to Brown, whose post route across the field split Dolphin safeties Sammy Knight and Brock Marion. Miami was in a two-deep zone. The Dolphins let Brown get too deep and he ended up scoring.

"Brady, I don't know how long he held onto the ball," Dolphins coach Dave Wannstedt said, "but he throws it on time, [Brown's] not going to get behind [the coverage]."

Brown, running out of "bunch" formations designed to prevent Miami's defenders from matching up with and pressing receivers, had 131 yards on six receptions. His touchdown was the longest reception of his 11-year career.

"Tom said, 'This is your play.' So I ran as hard as I could," Brown said. "I was tired of being out there. It was getting hot. Guys on defense were starting to cramp up. I wanted to finish it right there."

The Patriots looked done when Miami converted four third downs on a 16-play drive to what was assumed would be Mare's go-ahead field goal. But "Block Right Push" saved the day. They looked done again when Fiedler and Derrius Thompson hooked up on a questionable 31-yard completion on the second play of OT, and when Ricky Williams scooted for 10 and 13 yards on the next two plays to put Miami at New England's 20. But Mare was wide right.

It turned out they were never out. Most important, not at halftime (10-6, Miami), the way they were last year (16-0). "We knew coming in if we just fought them for 60 minutes—actually, today was 60-plus—we could pull it out," Woody said. "We just kept slugging it out and eventually came out winners."

SACKS	PENALTIES	TIME OF POSSESSION	RECORD
1 | 1	5 | 4	34:45 | 34:30	5-2 | 4-2

LOSING VIEWS
Olindo Mare (above) failed to convert with his chances to win the game then watched as the Patriots' offense and defense finished off Jay Fiedler & Co.

**WINNNING
GRABS**
Tedy Bruschi
tormented Jay
Fiedler through-
out the game then
celebrated with
Troy Brown and
teammates after
the victory.

☆ ★ ★ ☆ ★ ★ ★ ★ ★ ☆ ☆ ☆ ☆ ☆ ☆

BROWNS

9-3

FOXBOROUGH

OCTOBER 26
2003

62 DEGREES
DRIZZLE

Brown baggers

by MICHAEL SMITH

HALFWAY THROUGH THE REGULAR SEASON, the time had come for the bruised and battered Patriots to finally catch a break.

They got it in the form of a Cleveland team whose preferred quarterback, Kelly Holcomb, has a broken right fibula—a bleeding broken right fibula, actually—so painful he could not start, though he was pressed into action when starter Tim Couch sprained his right thumb near the end of the first half. A team without its stud running back, former Boston College star William Green, who sat with an injured right shoulder. A team without three of its opening-day starters on the offensive line. "Join the club, buddy," Tedy Bruschi said. "It's not a matter of who's down but who's in there and are they getting the job done."

That, in a nutshell, is the story of New England's season, one that at the midpoint has them 6-2 for the fifth time in franchise history and leading the AFC East. Getting the job done in the 9-3 win was Kevin Faulk, who contributed 154 yards from scrimmage, a career-high 96 rushing. Putting in work was second-year tight end Daniel Graham with seven catches for 110 yards, easily the best game of his career. Owed time and a half is a New England defense that allowed Cleveland to reach midfield twice and has allowed one touchdown in its last three games. Earning his check was Mike Vrabel with a career-high three sacks and a forced fumble against the team he grew up supporting. Em-

EYES WIDE SHUT
Soggy weather didn't keep the Patriots for opening holes for a career-best rushing day by Kevin Faulk.

FIRST DOWNS	RUSHING YARDS	PASSING YARDS	TURNOVERS
NE 19 | 13 CLE	94 | 84	253 | 119	0 | 1

SACKS	PENALTIES	TIME OF POSSESSION	RECORD
4 | 1	5 | 3	33:09 | 26:51	6-2 | 3-5

ployee of the day: Special teams coach Brad Seely, whose unit accounted for all the Patriots' points and downed four Ken Walter punts inside the 20.

There are some concerns on this week's evaluation, namely the offense's struggles in the red zone (0 for 3) and on third down (4 for 14). But the crew won its fourth in a row and sixth in seven. Boss Belichick is pleased.

"That was really about the way we expected that game to go," Bill Belichick said of his second win in three tries against his former team, this one not a done deal until Ty Law intercepted Holcomb with less than a minute to go. "Cleveland is a team that has been in a lot of close games. That's usually what it comes down to and that's certainly what it came down to today—last possession of the game."

"Some of these weeks we're going to need to score a lot more points than we did," acknowledged Tom Brady, who got the offense to the doorstep of the red zone (the 20) late in the fourth quarter before looking to Vinatieri to salvage 3 from 38. "We had some opportunities, but we really just didn't take advantage. At some

point, that's going to bite you in the butt."

The defense, sparked by the return of Law and Willie McGinest and a career game by Akron, Ohio, native and former Ohio State standout Vrabel, saved the Patriots' rears by forcing punts on eight of Cleveland's 10 possessions and allowing only three of 14 third downs to be converted. The Browns employed a lot of three-receiver sets yet managed only 119 passing yards. The Patriots sacked Couch once and Holcomb thrice, and made the poor guy run around on those bad legs more than he would have liked.

"We put a lot into this game," Vrabel said. "We knew how important it was and what time in the season we were at where you could start to go one way or another. We knew it was important, with the schedule we had coming up. We needed to win this football game."

"We played a tough game, a physical game and just were able to keep the edge," Matt Light said. "It's not always going to be pretty out there. Those guys get paid to play, too."

But it was New England's guys who really earned their money yesterday. So much so that Boss Belichick gave them a day off.

FOOT-BALL
Adam Vinatieri (4) gave the Patriots all their points and received thanks from teammate Dan Koppen.

☆ ★ ☆ ★ ★ ★ ★ ★ ☆ ☆ ★ ☆ ☆ ☆

BRONCOS

DENVER

30-26

**NOVEMBER 3
2003**

**35 DEGREES
FOGGY**

High and mighty

by MICHAEL HOLLEY

SOME OF THE BIGGEST NAMES IN NFL HISTORY have been on his side in his career. Bill Belichick has coached Lawrence Taylor, been on staff with Bill Parcells, and befriended Jim Brown. He has witnessed a miracle team—the 2001 Patriots—raise a Lombardi Trophy to the sky.

But with all that said, his current team may be his favorite.

Play a close game in Miami? Please. They'd rather win on an 82-yard pass from Tom Brady to Troy Brown. Stay competitive against the Titans and Eagles? Sure. They'll take wins, too, blitzing on most defensive plays against Donovan McNabb and unleashing Mike Cloud (7 carries, 73 yards) on the Titans.

Against the Broncos, the Patriots were facing a team that has haunted them since the late 1960s, when Belichick was a student at Annapolis High School. The Broncos have humiliated the Patriots here and in Foxborough. They have beaten them with Craig Morton at quarterback, John Elway at quarterback, and Brian Griese at quarterback. On a night when Al Michaels, John Madden, and the rest of the nation was watching, the Patriots won, 30-26.

They won even though they were doing their own rendition of "Scary Movie 3" in the first half. The Broncos held the ball for more than 21 minutes to New England's eight, the Patri-

FIRST DOWNS	RUSHING YARDS	PASSING YARDS	TURNOVERS
NE 17 | 18 DEN	69 | 114	350 | 163	2 | 1

NO STRETCH
Deion Branch collected three
passes for 107 yards, including a
66-yarder for a touchdown.

SACKS	PENALTIES	TIME OF POSSESSION	OPPONENTS RECORD
0 0	14 4	28:26 31:24	7-2 5-4

GOOD CALL
A win in Denver
is enough to
make Bill
Belichick hug
offensive
coordinator
Charlie Weis.

ots had three first downs to the Broncos' 14, and the home team had run twice as many offensive plays.

The halftime score? Broncos, 17-13.

"I've got an empty spot in my heart right now," Broncos quarterback Danny Kanell said when the remarkable game was over. "In my mind, I thought we were going to win."

So, too, did most of the 76,203 fans at Invesco Field at Mile High. It didn't look great for the Patriots a couple hours before the game. That's

when the team announced that dominating defensive tackle/defensive end Richard Seymour did not travel with the team because of a leg injury.

It was going to be difficult enough facing Clinton Portis—averaging more than 5 yards per carry—with Seymour. But stopping him with two rookies (Dan Klecko and Ty Warren) holding down the interior seemed a lot to ask.

Portis ran for 111 yards and scored the Broncos' first touchdown, but he was controlled most of the night. His performance was good; the Patriots had someone on their side who was great.

Remember, this team's official bumper sticker is, "We go beyond what you expect." Brady was the embodiment of that slogan, opening the New England scoring with a 66-yard pass to Deion Branch.

The play was executed in typical Patriots style. While the highlight shows will focus on Brady-to-Branch, the play came to life because of the behind-the-scenes work of Troy Brown. Brown was able to sell safety Kenoy Kennedy on a short pass. Kennedy bit so hard on Brown's route that he wound up hitting the receiver about 15 yards from the line of scrimmage.

This is why this team is on its way to being Belichick's favorite. He is a cerebral sort, and he loves to be surrounded by football intellectuals. It is why he still talks reverentially about Taylor and his ability to figure out the techniques being used against him. It is why he has so much admiration for Jim Brown, who was not only a dominant fullback but a dominant lacrosse player as well. And it is why he appreciates the little things—Brown's route running, Adam Vinatieri's efficiency, Brady's hunger to be better—in his current team.

If you focus on the warts, the Patriots had no business winning the game. They were extremely sloppy, accumulating 14 penalties. But they offset the sloppiness with 350 yards from Brady, a game-changing special teams move in the fourth quarter, and a winning touchdown catch by receiver David Givens.

Trailing, 24-23, with 2:51 remaining and at their 1, Belichick and special teams coach Brad Seely agreed that long snapper Lonie Paxton should intentionally snap the ball out of the end zone. That gave the Broncos 2 points and a 26-23 lead, but it also gave New England a free kick. Ken Walter, who had a weak 20-yard punt earlier in the game, responded with a 64-yard boomer to the Denver 15. Thirty-four seconds later, the Patriots had the ball and were on their way to the winning drive.

The night ended when Brady hit Givens for an 18-yard touchdown pass over Deltha O'Neal.

There wasn't much noise in the Rockies after Givens made his catch. Mostly, you heard the sounds of jubilant men in silver helmets. Belichick didn't toss his headset in the air as he did in Miami, but he probably felt like it. The coach likes to listen to the Beatles and the Allmans and Jon Bon Jovi. This team is going to cause him to switch up his soundtrack. When he thinks of the '03 Patriots and what they've done, he might want to slide "My Favorite Things" into his compact disc player.

CLOSING STATEMENTS Tom Brady (above) leaves the field happy to have thrown a game-winning touchdown pass to David Givens (left).

71

☆ ★ ☆ ★ ★ ★ ★ ★ ★ ☆ ☆ ☆ ☆ ☆

COWBOYS

12-0

FOXBOROUGH

NE | DAL

NOVEMBER 16
2003

33 DEGREES
CLOUDY

Lone Star state

by MICHAEL SMITH

BEFORE THE GAME, NO MATTER HOW HARD BILL Belichick and Bill Parcells fought to escape the spotlight, it really was all about them. Do the two of you speak? Will you speak? How do you feel about Bill? And how do you feel about Bill? What did you learn from Bill? Are you still angry at Bill?

After the game, it was still all about them. Look, they hugged each other. What did he say? What did he say? What does this win mean to you, Bill? What does this loss mean to you, Bill?

In between, though, it really was all about the players. Just like the coaches said. And right now, Belichick has a better collection of them.

His Patriots improved to 8-2 for the second time in franchise history (1978) and maintained their two-game lead in the AFC East with a 12-0 victory over the Cowboys before a national television audience and 68,436 at Gillette Stadium. The shutout was New England's first since the third game of the 1996 season, when Parcells coached the Patriots and Belichick was his assistant, and the second time Dallas has been held scoreless in its last four games.

The Cowboys amassed more total yards and held a slight edge in time of possession, but they turned the ball over three times, once inside the Patriots 20. Tom Brady completed just 15 of 34 passes, but completions of 57 yards to David Givens and 46 yards to Deion Branch led to 9 points. His counterpart, Quincy Carter, threw three interceptions, including one in the third quarter to Ty Law with Dallas 19 yards away from making it a 2-point game.

And yes, they did embrace. "Bill congratulated

FIRST DOWNS	RUSHING YARDS	PASSING YARDS	TURNOVERS
NE 14 | 17 DAL	65 | 84	203 | 207	1 | 3

CLOSING STATEMENTS
Tom Brady (above) leaves the field happy to have thrown a game-winning touchdown pass to David Givens (below).

SACKS	PENALTIES	TIME OF POSSESSION	OPPONENTS RECORD
1|2	7|10	29:14|30:46	8-2|7-3

me on the win," Belichick said. "I told him I thought he had a good football team and I wished him well, and I do."

And as far as Belichick was concerned, thus ended the Battle of the Bills. "Coach Belichick told us to enjoy this win," said Ty Law, who had two interceptions, "but he reminded us that Houston is a tough team. They went up there to Buffalo and did something we didn't do, and that's beat those guys [12-10]."

"All the players knew this was big for him," guard Damien Woody said. "We're happy for him. It's one more step in the right direction for the organization."

"It's good to beat the teacher," said defensive coordinator Romeo Crennel, also a former Parcells employee. "We feel good about that. But our main focus is that we have to go to Houston next week."

The Cowboys offense had its share of problems. Dallas managed a mere 3 yards per carry and Carter struggled to a 38.0 quarterback rating. New England's defense did a lot less bending than usual.

"They played a lot better than we did," Parcells said. "We just didn't give ourselves a chance to win the game. I thought maybe there in the third quarter, where we had that one decent drive in there, if we could have got on the board there,

we might have made it close. As it happened all night, we just kind of self-destructed."

"We just tried to play physical, tried to get up in [Terry Glenn's] face and attack him at the line of scrimmage," Law said, applying New England's general game plan specifically to his former teammate and friend. "You don't want to let him find soft spots in the zone. Because once he gets running, it's probably going to be hard to catch him. Granted, he's probably faster than the majority of us out there; we have to stop him any way we can. The only way you can beat speed is with strength, and that's the way you hold the guy down."

"It was a shot game," said Givens, who missed most of the second half with a right leg injury. "Whoever hit the most shots would win the game, and we hit the most shots."

Brady hit one in the first quarter to Branch, who came free (thanks to a pick by Givens) across the middle for a 46-yard catch-and-run. Four plays later, Adam Vinatieri kicked a 23-yard field goal for a 3-0 lead. Vinatieri kicked a 26-yarder just after the 2-minute warning for the game's final points.

Law intercepted Carter in the end zone on the game's final play, Carter's second pick of the fourth quarter (Tyrone Poole).

Said Belichick, "We just find a way to win."

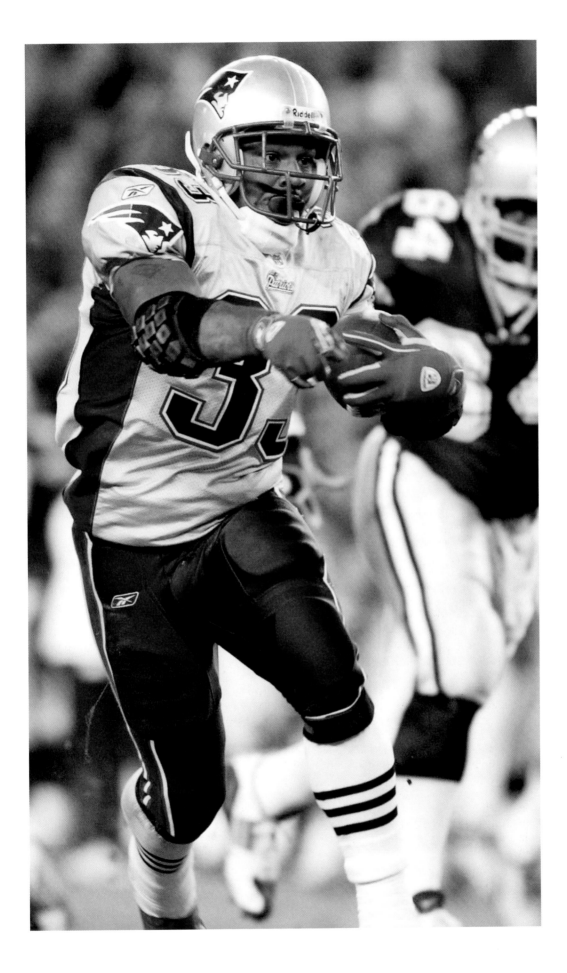

TO THE POINT
Kevin Faulk
breaks free from
the Dallas
defense — if only
for a moment.

☆ ★ ★ ☆ ★ ★ ★ ★ ★ ★ ★ ★ ☆ ☆ ☆ ☆

TEXANS

23-20

HOUSTON

NOVEMBER 23
2003

INDOORS

In the end, it's Brady

by DAN SHAUGHNESSY

TOUGH FEW DAYS FOR TOM BRADY. HIS APART-ment was burglarized and he lost a television. Two of his passes were stolen by the Texans and he lost a fumble. He also got pancaked near his own end zone in overtime.

But he's Tom Brady and somewhere along the line the football gods sprinkled stardust on his shoulder pads. There's always another TV to be delivered and there's always another victory to be won after the game appears lost. When you are Tom Brady the road of landmines always leads to somewhere over the rainbow.

In yet another seemingly hopeless late-game situation yesterday, Brady overcame some un-characteristic mistakes and led the Patriots to a 23-20 OT victory over the Houston Texans before 70,719 ten-gallon-mad-hatters at Reliant Stadi-um. Brady's gaudy numbers included 29 com-pletions in 47 attempts for a whopping 368 yards and two touchdowns, but those don't real-ly tell you much about what kind of a day this was for QB 12.

This was a game in which Brady made some old-fashioned Bledsoe-like blunders—trying to do too much when he'd have been better off eat-ing the football. It was a game in which the Pa-triots annihilated the Texans in every offensive category except points. Brady gets much of the blame for the shortcomings, but he scrambled when he had to scramble, and converted third-down and fourth-down plays in the fourth quar-ter and OT when he had to make them, and somehow he willed his team to victory. Again. With Brady at quarterback, the Patriots are 7-0 in overtime games.

"It didn't look good there for a while," he said. "But it showed you we've got a lot of heart and perseverance."

After a day of mistakes and failure to capital-ize, the Patriots trailed, 20-13, and faced a third-and-10 from their 33 with 2:26 left when Brady dropped back to pass and saw nothing. His miniature receivers were all covered and there were linemen in his face. At that moment, he did something very un-Brady like. He scrambled.

Brady is not Doug Flutie. Brady scrambling looks as natural as Bob Kraft dancing with Ty Law at City Hall Plaza. But he eluded his pur-suers and gave Daniel Graham time to get open. He finally got it to Graham downfield for a game-saving 33-yard completion.

"I was running for my life," Brady said. "The first couple of guys weren't open. I had to spin back and roll to my right. I saw Daniel lose his guy and I just threw it. I didn't see the comple-tion."

The big gain set up (five plays later) a fourth-and-1 4-yard touchdown pass to Graham with 40 seconds left that sent the game into OT. The TD required more improvisation from New Eng-land's signal-caller. He ran a bootleg to his right, but the Texans hadn't gone for the fake run to the left and it was clear Brady was going to lose his footrace for the first down. Instead of letting the game end on the play, he threw off his back foot, against the flow, and lofted it over coverage and into the suddenly dependable hands of Gra-ham.

In OT, Brady could have lost the game again, but somehow he held on to the ball when he was blindsided by Jamie Sharper on a third-and-6 from his 13. A fumble would have meant the end of New England's six-game winning streak, but Brady held on, the Patriots punted, and they lived for another possession.

On the winning drive, Brady took the Patriots

FIRST DOWNS	RUSHING YARDS	PASSING YARDS	TURNOVERS
NE 29 | 11 HOU	128 | 89	344 | 80	3 | 2

HANDY ENDING
After a rough week at home and a tough game in Houston, Tom Brady was a cool customer in overtime.

SACKS	PENALTIES	TIME OF POSSESSION	RECORD
3 | 4	5 | 6	43:50 | 30:29	9-2 | 4-7

OOPS
The unsure hands of Daniel
Graham provided clutch grabs
later against the Texans.

from their 14 down to the Houston 10, setting up Adam Vinatieri's field goal with just 41 seconds left in OT. The win gave Brady a career regular-season record (as a starter) of 29-12, which leads all active quarterbacks.

The win pushed New England to 9-2 for the first time in franchise history, but the Patriots know they won't be able to make so many mistakes (a blocked field goal and punt to go with Brady's gaffes) if they plan to return to Houston for Super Bowl XXXVIII Feb. 1.

"Tom tried to make a play and sometimes you just get hit," said coach Bill Belichick. "I'm sure Tom would like it back. But a game like his comes down to big plays, and whoever makes them deserves to win. Tom has always been great at the end of games. He's a good decision-maker. He really did a good job."

By Brady's lofty standards, it was not a particularly good job, despite the hefty numbers. A team doesn't usually win when its QB turns it over three times.

But this is 2003. This is Tom Brady. The Patriots always win. Next time they play here they'll be representing the AFC, maybe dressing in the home team's locker room.

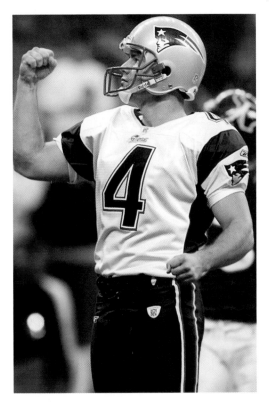

SECOND CHANCE
Adam Vinatieri had one field goal blocked but he was on target when it counted in overtime.

GAME 12

☆ ★ ☆ ★ ★ ★ ★ ★ ★ ★ ★ ★ ★ ☆ ☆ ☆

COLTS

INDIANAPOLIS

38-34

NOVEMBER 30
2003

INDOORS

Magic carpet ride

by MICHAEL HOLLEY

IT'S GOING TO BE CAPTURED IN PICTURES AND songs. It's going to be the centerpiece of the Patriots' 2003 highlight video. It's going to have its own sponsorship deal. It just may be stolen in the middle of the night and passed around like a Stanley Cup.

Is it really possible for a single yard—36 inches of RCA Dome carpet—to be famous?

At the end of their draining afternoon against the Indianapolis Colts, the Patriots learned a lot about themselves. They realized that they are vulnerable enough to be shoved to the ledge. But if you're going to knock them off it, you'll need to use two forceful hands and prevent them from so much as a sliver on which to hang.

And 36 inches is far too much space.

The Patriots were able to win their 10th game of the season, 38-34, because they refused to give Edgerrin James a hole to run through. With 40 seconds remaining and the Colts with a first down at the Patriots' 2, James ran for a yard.

He tried to run up the middle on second down, and he was stopped for no gain. On third down, Peyton Manning tried to pass his way into the end zone and couldn't find rookie receiver Aaron Moorehead. On fourth down, with just 14 seconds left, the home team found itself in a strange land.

The Colts were going to be running, but they were in a passing formation. They had three receivers on the field, and the Patriots were in man-to-man coverage. Someone, either a line-

FIRST DOWNS		RUSHING YARDS	PASSING YARDS	TURNOVERS
NE 21	26 IND	56 98	226 272	3 2

SHOW STOPPERS
Eugene Wilson (26) and Willie McGinest (55) helped the Patriots to clamp down on a final rush by the high-scoring Indy offense.

SACKS	PENALTIES	TIME OF POSSESSION	RECORD
2	2	6	4	27:59	32:01	10-2	9-3

HAPPY RETURNS, 1 Bethel Johnson avoids a tackle and stays inbounds on his way to a half-ending kickoff return for a touchdown.

backer or a safety, was going to be unblocked.

That someone turned out to be outside linebacker Willie McGinest, who dropped James for a 1-yard loss. The game was over, and the Patriots were out of town with their eighth consecutive win.

One yard is the obvious difference between winning and losing, but it represents other things as well. It is the difference between sleeping at home and sleeping in a place where you have to dial 9 for an outside line. It's the difference between Gillette Stadium and the RCA Dome in January. It's the difference between

Quincy Market and Market Square, the Mass. Pike and the Indiana Toll Road.

The Patriots now own "quality" wins over the Titans, Colts, Eagles, Cowboys, and Dolphins. Those teams are a combined 43-16. The Patriots are a playoff team that has beaten playoff teams. Their hyper defense of that 1-yard green space helps them get a little closer to playing a postseason game—or games—at home.

It's becoming more difficult to look elsewhere for the best team in the AFC. Since the Patriots have a few glaring blemishes, it can't be them, right? They have a modern-day Tony Nathan

(Kevin Faulk) as their most productive runner, Mike Cloud leads them in touchdowns with five, and Antowain Smith, one of the quiet heroes of Super Bowl XXXVI, was deactivated for yesterday's game.

When they needed to run out the clock with a late lead, the Patriots couldn't do it. Faulk fumbled with 3:53 left to set up a field goal that made it 38-34. On the next series, the Patriots burned just 20 seconds because they were forced to throw when they wanted to run.

And we haven't even talked about the struggles of punter Ken Walter.

But as Belichick said when asked about Walter yesterday, "What's out there?" What team is out there that should frighten New England?

If you mention playoffs to the head coach and his players, they'll all deflect the compliment and try to reroute the conversation. They don't spend a lot of time, publicly, dwelling on where they now stand. No one could have imagined that in September, when we were talking about one big cut—of Lawyer Milloy—instead of one big yard.

There is no doubt that the Patriots are enthusiastic this morning. They tend to put on tragedy masks to keep themselves humble, but everyone who is paying attention can see the smiles.

Yeah, they blew a 21-point lead. Yeah, Tom Brady seemed to lose his touch in the second half after completing 20 of his first 23 passes. Yeah, Manning had them retreating until the final minute.

The Patriots, though, are a proud group. Everyone who spoke yesterday talked of toughness and resolve. They know they would never allow themselves to make the excuses the Colts did following their remake of "The Longest Yard." The Colts said they couldn't get into their goal-line offense because they didn't have their regular personnel.

No, the New Englanders would have come up with something. That's what they've been doing all year.

Before Belichick left the dome, he was asked about the plane ride home. He laughed. He allowed a peek into his thoughts, saying the mood was so light that "we don't need a plane to get back."

HAPPY RETURNS, 2 Bethel Johnson gets free for another long kickoff return against the Colts.

DOLPHINS

12-0

FOXBOROUGH

DECEMBER 7
2003

28 DEGREES
SNOW

Snowballin' into the playoffs

by MICHAEL SMITH

SUCCESS WON'T CHANGE THE PATRIOTS. BETTER yet, success in December won't change the Patriots. "We've got big plans," said rookie safety Eugene Wilson. "[This is] the first step."

New England secured its second AFC East title in three seasons with a 12-0 win over the Miami Dolphins at a giant snow globe commonly known as Gillette Stadium.

If the players celebrated over any of this, they kept it brief and conducted it before outsiders were allowed into their locker room. They left the fun to the 45,378 fans, who following Tedy Bruschi's fourth-quarter touchdown used the snow that caused major logistical problems for party favors, tossing it skyward in unison. Honestly, the only visible proof that the players had accomplished anything was their commemorative T-shirts.

Blame it on Bill Belichick. The coach's tunnel-vision approach has seen the Patriots through 11 victories in 12 games and nine consecutive wins, so who are we to suggest correction? In the postgame locker room, he congratulated his team, told it to savor its first season sweep of Miami since 1997.

"Everything trickles down from Coach Belichick," said Antowain Smith, who went from the inactive list to carrying 27 times. "He's not going to let us get too high. The main thing he told us was to be humble, that it's a great victory for us, and not to take anything away from ourselves. But the job is not complete yet."

"He keeps putting goals up there for you," offensive lineman Damien Woody said. "You nev-

FIRST DOWNS	RUSHING YARDS	PASSING YARDS	TURNOVERS
NE 13 | 7 MIA	78 | 68	150 | 66	1 | 3

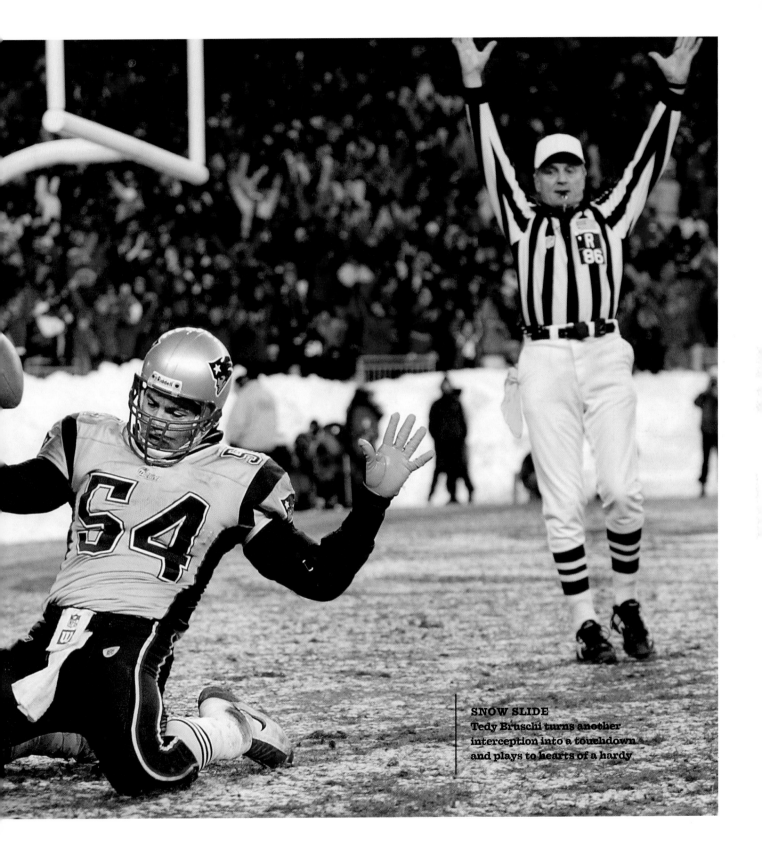

SNOW SLIDE
Tedy Bruschi turns another interception into a touchdown and plays to hearts of a hardy

SACKS	PENALTIES	TIME OF POSSESSION	RECORD
5|3	2|4	32:45|27:15	11-2|8-5

er want to stay the same. You want to keep going up. He always puts goals in front of us. Even after a victory like this, the goal now is to maintain the No. 1 seed and beat a Jacksonville squad that's on the rise."

Belichick did not entertain any discussion before the game about the possibility that his team would clinch a division title sooner than any other in franchise history. After it was done, he had little to say about it.

"It's one of your goals at the beginning of the year," said Belichick, whose team is tied with the 2001 edition for the most regular-season wins in Patriots history. "We're happy about it, obviously, but there's still a lot of football left to be played this year. We'll just keep looking ahead. I saw Jacksonville had a really big win and I watched a little bit of them on tape week. They're pretty good, especially defensively. This will be a good challenge for us. We have to put this one behind us and move ahead. We'll enjoy it for a couple of hours."

It was not any enjoyable three hours for Miami, the fifth opponent New England has held to 10 points or fewer this season and the second straight visitor to Gillette Stadium not to score. (Tennessee's Steve McNair, four home games and two months ago, was the last person to score a touchdown here.) If you don't think this season is special, consider that the Patriots, coming into the season, had not shut out an opponent since 1996.

The Patriots held Miami's offense to 134 yards and an average of 2.2 yards per play. They sacked Jay Fiedler five times and forced him into 13-for-31 passing, with two interceptions. Ricky Williams gained 68 yards on 25 carries. They forced a Dolphins-record 11 punts by Matt Turk.

New England's offense didn't do much, either. Tom Brady and Co. did what they had to, and that was plenty. They held the ball for 32 minutes, 45 seconds. "I certainly didn't think we racked up many statistics," said Brady (16 of 31, 163 yards, 6 completions each to Deion Branch and Daniel Graham). "There weren't many mistakes, and I think a lot of times we play to the score, and we were winning."

The offense produced Adam Vinatieri's 29-yard field goal 13:14 into the first period. The defense did the rest—Bruschi's 5-yard interception return for a touchdown with about 9 minutes remaining, and Jarvis Green's sack of Fiedler for safety with 1:13 left.

Bruschi has returned his last four interceptions for touchdowns. "It was defense where we had all the guys covered up. I peeked at Jay's eyes and there was the ball right there. I had to reach up and grab it."

And the fans proceeded to grab and toss what was left of the estimated 30 inches of snow Foxborough received over the weekend. "That was incredible, wasn't it?" Bruschi said. "Throwing the snow up in the air with the music. It got me into the holiday spirit."

JAGUARS

27-13

FOXBOROUGH

DECEMBER 14
2003

25 DEGREES
SNOW

Some of everything

by MICHAEL HOLLEY

TWELVE AND TWO IS NICE, BUT IT DOESN'T BEGIN to tell their story. The Patriots aren't just a team sitting atop a division, conference, and league. They really are a group that's big enough and diverse enough to represent an entire six-state region.

This is the team for accountants, mathematicians, and all those who see beauty in numbers. This is the team for dreamers. This is the team for streakers (no, not that kind). This is the team for serious thinkers, motivators, practical jokers, and even gifted students who sometimes lose their focus.

All of this—and a bunch of snow—was on display again at Gillette Stadium. Jacksonville was in town, and the Jaguars' logo became the latest symbolic brick to be placed in the stadium walls. The Patriots won, 27-13, to push their winning streak to 10.

Their 10-game streak is the longest in team history. Their 12 wins are the most in team history. They have allowed 22 points in their last five home games, which is one of the best defensive runs in any team's history. They have allowed 68 points at home, and 30 of those came in one game.

At times, the Patriot coaches must feel like teachers trying to come up with a demanding curriculum. Bill Belichick and his staff are constantly challenging the players to achieve a goal that has eluded them.

Some of the targets are obvious (win the game, don't turn over the ball). Others are directed at specific game situations. One of the Patriot challenges was to score on the opening drive. After about five minutes and 66 yards, the team had wiped another item from the coaches' charts.

FIRST DOWNS	RUSHING YARDS	PASSING YARDS	TURNOVERS
NE 18 | 17 JAX	84 | 72	212 | 282	1 | 2

GOOD HANDS
Rookie David Givens shows why his hands are becoming dependable targets for Tom Brady.

SACKS	PENALTIES	TIME OF POSSESSION	RECORD
1 | 2	4 | 8	32:41 | 27:19	12-2 | 4-10

TOO SOON
Premature celebration kept Tyrone Poole from finishing off this interception return with a touchdown dance.

But there's always something.

As much as Belichick enjoys leading a team with 12 wins, he is forever fearful of complacency and arrogance. The coach counts Jim Brown as a close friend; you would have thought he was talking about Brown when he described Jaguars running back Fred Taylor before this game. Most fans probably have noticed how much Belichick has downplayed wins lately.

Remember, this was the same man who threw his headphones in the air in Miami and was extremely complimentary of everyone in Denver. Not now. He knows there are fewer dissenting national voices when it comes to the Patriots. He knows that his players can't sing the "nobody believed in us" refrain, because it seems that everyone believes lately.

So when there is even the slightest sign of a lapse, he reacts. Rookie receiver Bethel Johnson did not have a strong week of practice, so he was inactive for yesterday's game. Belichick is intrigued by Johnson's speed and potential, but not intrigued enough to put Johnson on the field when he is drifting during practice.

The coach is a fan of Tyrone Poole, who has played like a Pro Bowler at cornerback. But Poole realizes that some coach may make an example out of him. Poole intercepted two passes. On his second pick, he had a 44-yard return and appeared to be headed for a touchdown. He held the ball up near the 5, thinking he had a clear path to the end zone.

He didn't.

He was tackled at the 3.

An interviewer asked him if the name Leon Lett sounded familiar. He smiled. Lett is the former Cowboys defensive lineman who celebrated a touchdown too early in the Super Bowl and had the ball stripped from him on the way to a score.

"I didn't fumble," Poole said. "I wasn't in the same area [with Lett]. I may be the next-door neighbor, but I'm not in the same house."

Belichick has been known to use books (Sun Tzu's "Art of War"), songs, and videos to motivate his team. He'll be at it again for the next of couple weeks. He knows what's in front of his team now: a chance to win out and, ultimately, secure the right to play in the sloppy weather of the Northeast.

This team doesn't view The Streak as a streak. It sees the game as one episode out of 16.

In the latest episode, the Patriots held Taylor to 57 quiet yards. They got touchdowns from Troy Brown and Daniel Graham. They got an efficient game from Tom Brady. They proved once again that they know what they're doing, even when they are playing in snow.

These Patriots, built by white-collar workers and sustained by blue-collar employees, truly belong to the region. Yesterday, for the 10th consecutive game, they produced an episode that was an all-ages show.

JETS

EAST RUTHERFORD,
NEW JERSEY

21-16

DECEMBER 20
2003

30 DEGREES
CLEAR

☆ ★ ★ ☆ ★ ★ ★ ★ ★ ★ ★ ★ ★ ★ ★ ☆

Eleventh hour

by MICHAEL SMITH

BASED ON THE HISTORY OF THIS SERIES, IF there was a game that posed the biggest threat to the Patriots' winning streak, "Jets at the Meadowlands" was the one.

The threat was real, but the streak remains intact.

The 2003 Patriots extended their franchise record with their 11th straight, a 21-16 takedown of the Jets before a national television audience and 77,835 at the Meadowlands.

It was again the Patriots defense that made the difference. The Patriots intercepted Jets quarterback Chad Pennington five times, including one that Willie McGinest returned 15 yards for a touchdown in the second quarter that gave the Patriots' a lead they would hold for the rest of the evening. Another of Pennington's picks, by Tedy Bruschi, led to New England's first touchdown. Still another, Ty Law's pick in the end zone in the third quarter, ended a Jets scoring threat. Safeties Rodney Harrison and Eugene Wilson also had interceptions.

"Getting those scores early, that was important," coach Bill Belichick said. "We were able to play most of the game from ahead, which was good."

Bruschi's leaping interception over the middle on New York's second play from scrimmage gave the Patriots possession at the Jets' 35. On the next play, Tom Brady and David Givens collaborated on a 35-yard touchdown, giving the Patriots a 7-0 lead 48 seconds into the game.

New England did not score a touchdown on its first possession in its first 13 games. The Patriots have done it two weeks in a row.

Givens would later catch his team-leading fifth touchdown of the season, a 5-yarder on the first drive of the third quarter.

The Patriots' early lead didn't last long, however. Actually, it did. About 9:20. Pennington responded by directing the Jets on a 16-play, 83-yard drive that ended with his 1-yard touchdown run. The Patriots had the play-action pass cov-ered well on third and goal but Pennington kept rolling out until he reached the end zone.

McGinest broke the 7-7 tie with his interception return 1:26 into the second quarter. On third and 2 from his 15, Pennington tried to hit Curtis Conway on a slant. McGinest, in perfect position, used his 6-foot-5-inch frame to leap and deflect the pass. A la Asante Samuel in Game 3, McGinest caught the deflection and took it to the end zone. It was the Patriots' league-leading sixth defensive touchdown this season.

With 1:55 to go before intermission, the Jets took over at their 25. Eighty-four seconds later, they were at New England's 5, but the Jets had to settle for Doug Brien's 29-yard field goal and a 4-point deficit at halftime.

Pennington, who scored both New York touchdowns on runs of 1 and 10 yards, never had thrown more than two interceptions in any of his first 26 games (19 starts). The Jets' five turnovers equaled a third of their giveaways through their first 14 games—15, the second fewest in the league.

The previous time the Patriots faced Pennington, he picked them apart, passing for 285 yards and three touchdowns. That was last year, before Bill Belichick overhauled his secondary. In the rematch, Pennington just got picked. And picked. And picked.

"We tried to disguise a lot, move around a lot," Harrison said. "To be honest with you, you can disguise all you want against good quarterbacks, but it comes down to guys making plays."

Antowain Smith carried 18 times for a season-high 121 yards—New England's first 100-yard rusher in 22 games. Smith broke runs of 30 and 23 yards, his longest of the season.

"It's all about attitude," Damien Woody said. "That's one area they're deficient at on defense, is rush defense [31st in the league coming into the game], so that's one area you want to go after them in. Everybody across the board did a good job of getting after guys."

	FIRST DOWNS			RUSHING YARDS		PASSING YARDS		TURNOVERS
NE	13	22	NJY	133	109	138	212	1 5

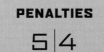

MAKING A POINT
Willie McGinest celebrates his
touchdown after intercepting a
pass–one of five by the Patriots.

SACKS	PENALTIES	TIME OF POSSESSION	RECORD
4 | 0	5 | 4	27:21 | 32:39	13-2 | 6-9

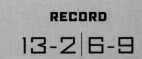

GAME 16

BILLS

31-0

BILLS

FOXBOROUGH

DECEMBER 27
2003

42 DEGREES
SUNNY

☆ ★ ★ ☆ ★ ★ ★ ★ ★ ★ ★ ★ ★ ★ ★ ★

A perfect finish

by NICK CAFARDO

ON A ROLL
Daniel Graham comes down with a touchdown catch during the regular-season finale.

HOME-FIELD ADVANTAGE THROUGHOUT THE playoffs. Revenge. Offensive and defensive domination. An 8-0 record at Gillette Stadium. A 14-2 regular-season record.

The closest thing to a perfect season, and the Patriots' best regular season ever, concluded at Gillette Stadium yesterday with a poetic 31-0 splattering of the Buffalo Bills. Buffalo appeared to pack it in even before the opening whistle and never challenged the Patriots, who won their 12th straight game.

The score was sweet revenge, matching the Week 1 thrashing of the Patriots by the Bills.

The Patriots' third shutout of the season was preserved by a Larry Izzo interception of Bills backup quarterback Travis Brown in the end zone with 13 seconds remaining.

"All 53 guys wanted to keep that zero on the scoreboard," said Izzo. "You have to give credit to everyone in this locker room. It wasn't just one play. It was 60 minutes of football."

There was no Gatorade splash of coach Bill Belichick late in the game. There was no large celebration in the locker room. This is a team that knows that if it doesn't win the Super Bowl, the regular season doesn't mean much.

The game showed the opposite paths former teammates Tom Brady and Drew Bledsoe are on. Bledsoe was 12 for 29 for 83 yards with one interception. Brady was 21 for 32 for 204 yards and threw four touchdowns in the first half. It was a rather sad performance by Bledsoe (34.7 rating in the game), one of the troika of personalities who saved Patriots football in the early '90s along with owner Robert Kraft and former Patriots coach Bill Parcells.

"Some people might look at the scoreboard and say Buffalo laid down. They fought hard and we whupped them," said Patriots linebacker Matt Chatham.

If that was the case on the field, it didn't look that way from afar. It looked like Bledsoe was on

FIRST DOWNS		RUSHING YARDS	PASSING YARDS	TURNOVERS
NE 26 | 16 BUF		131 | 82	190 | 174	1 | 4

an island, and the New England defense was in a feeding frenzy. It held the Bills to 256 yards and the time of possession was almost seven minutes in New England's favor.

Already trailing, 7-0, Bledsoe was hit as he threw his first pass of the game when Tedy Bruschi roared in on a blitz. Bledsoe's dying quail was picked off by Mike Vrabel and returned 14 yards to the Bills 34.

From there, the Patriots scored their second touchdown on a 9-yard pass from Brady to Bethel Johnson.

"It all happened pretty fast," said Johnson, the rookie who became one of Brady's favorite targets. "I don't know what coverage they were in, but they were pretty much leaving me out there by myself the whole time. Tom just recognized it and threw it on in."

OUT LOUD
A third home shutout was one of many things inspiring the Patriots' defense and Tedy Bruschi.

SACKS	PENALTIES	TIME OF POSSESSION	RECORD
4|2	4|10	33:08|26:52	14-2|6-10

The Players

Putting it together

As a team, the Patriots were the best the NFL has seen in a long time: the winning streak, the defense, the clutch plays. It was fashionable to describe them as a team whose total was greater than the sum of its parts.

But in many ways that would be a disservice to the parts and the man who put them together. Coach Bill Belichick, long labeled a "defensive mind," showed again that he has a keen eye for talent and how to build a team.

He knew that Tom Brady had the makings of a quarterback, that while not always flashy, would make the big plays in the big games and avoid the critical mistakes.

He knew how to get the best out of veterans like Ty Law, Willie McGinest and Tedy Bruschi and how to develop a rising star in Richard Seymour.

He knew how to find players like Rodney Harrison this seasonr and Mike Vrabel in 2001 from other teams that would be a good fit with the Patriots and put them over the top.

And he knew when to stay with a player like Adam Vinatieri who may have struggled at times but would be clutch in the playoffs.

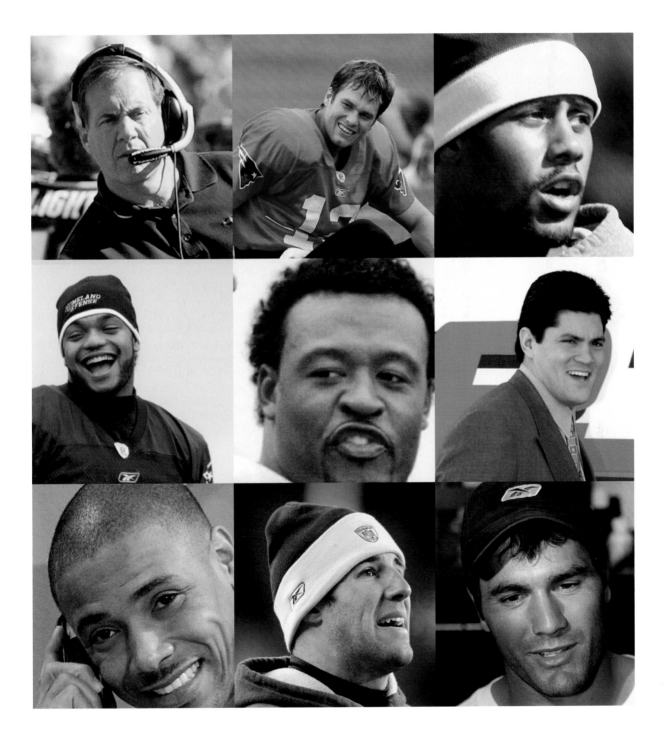

Bill Belichick

More than Xs and Os

by MICHAEL HOLLEY

The lights in the room aren't always dimmed, the seats aren't always theater-style, and the clicker isn't always in his right hand. As talented as Bill Belichick is in places where football films are studied, the head coach of the Patriots didn't become who he is by spending all his time in the dark.

He is more A to Z than X and O.

He is the prankster who once hid a slice of pizza in Scott Pioli's desk drawer. That was when he worked for the New York Jets and a group of guys—Belichick, Pioli, Berj Najarian, Mike Tannenbaum—were all in an office competition to drop a couple pounds. They had official weigh-ins and everything. To get a competitive advantage, Belichick tried to tempt Pioli with the scent of a delicious pie.

He is the kid from Annapolis, Md., who still smiles when talking about his odd jobs in his hometown. He worked for a moving company. He was a busboy getting generous tips at a restaurant, Middleton's Tavern, overlooking the city docks. He was a caddie who, if you listen to his father, was unlucky enough to chase down the errant shots of Spiro Agnew. Agnew, a Maryland native, was the state's governor who eventually became vice president of the United States.

"Spiro was an awful golfer," Steve Belichick said recently. "And he was cheap as hell."

He is the serious music fan who doesn't have a predictable listening pattern. Walk by his office on some days and you'll hear Tina Turner. His collection includes the Beatles, Santana, U2, Bob Dylan, and his friend, Jon Bon Jovi.

"Bill is a closet drummer," said Bon Jovi, who should know: he purchased a stylish drum kit for his friend. He also wrote the song "Bounce" because he said he was inspired by Belichick's resiliency.

The two talk often. Bon Jovi even sends ad-

vanced copies of his releases to Foxborough so the coach can review them.

"I think he enjoys getting the early copies," Bon Jovi said. "I can tell if he really likes a song, because he'll want to talk about it a lot. If he doesn't like it, he won't say, 'Jon, that's not so hot.' He just won't talk about it as much. That's how I know."

He is the son who followed the path of his father. Everyone knows that. Steve Belichick is a coach and so is his only child. But how many times have you heard someone say Bill Belichick also followed the path of his mother?

He did.

Jeanette Belichick is a gifted educator who met her husband at Hiram College in Ohio. She was a language instructor there; he was a football coach. At one time—when she says she was still in practice—she had an understanding of seven languages.

Her mind is sharp and curious. There are pictures of Bill, mementos, and NFL game balls on the mantel in Steve and Jeanette's Annapolis home. But there are books everywhere. Jeanette is a longtime reader of The New Yorker and has back issues stacked in the basement. She considered canceling her subscription once, when she believed the magazine became too risque under the leadership of Tina Brown. She softened when David Remnick took over.

It will take a special cook to match her in the kitchen. Her husband is willing to drive 10 or 15 miles away from their home to get a deal on crabcakes because he loves the way she prepares them. He likes the way she thinks, too.

She was the one who told Steve to rewrite his book on football scouting because it contained too much technical language. He initially disagreed and then conceded she was right.

Like her son, Jeanette Belichick cringes at the thought of uninspired or improper instruction.

"I'm telling you, I'm No. 3 in our family when it comes to brains," Steve Belichick said. "And

"You see all these old coaches wearing their (Super Bowl) rings. You're more likely to see Bill's boys wearing his ring than him." JON BON JOVI

I'm a distant third. My wife and son are kicking dust in my face. I used to be able to say I was No. 1 in football, but I can't even say that anymore."

Oh, football.

Bill Belichick is the football coach who always seemed to have the temperament and mentality for the job. His fascination with breaking down film at a young age is just part of the story.

There were early indications that Belichick was a step ahead of everyone else, even if he wound up taking some of those steps unwittingly. It didn't take the football coach and schoolteacher long to notice how quickly their son absorbed information.

The family used to spend winters in Florida and summers in Ohio. With lots of time to drive, they would play recognition games with their son on the road. Buicks, and Chryslers, and Fords would pass them on the highway and the parents would point out the different cars to their child.

After a few minutes, he would point out cars to them a few seconds before they could see them. That was one clue. The deep football comprehension as a preteen was another clue. Yet another one was the sound logic that always appeared to be at work. The parents would ask

their son a question and he always seemed to have an answer and an explanation for why he thought the way he did.

He was an excellent student and an enthusiastic sportsman. He played golf. He played football. He played lacrosse. During one of his last trips to Annapolis, Belichick was told that several of his lacrosse sticks were still scattered about the house. The sticks were there because the coach-to-be used to take broken equipment—his and his teammates'—and fix it at home.

Those days may have somehow prepared him for coaching, but his junior high and high school days provided the most significant groundwork. He went to school in the 1960s, when the country had violence—philosophical and physical—over civil rights.

Belichick was part of the first integrated classes at Annapolis High. He saw then how damaging it was to divide the country—and, in his case, the neighborhood—along racial lines. He was the son of an educator. He was the son of a Navy man who, at the end of World War II, roomed with an officer named Sam Barnes. That was unusual because Barnes, an Oberlin College graduate, was a black man and Steve Belichick, obviously, was not.

"I remember a lot of people asking me at the time what it was like to room with a black man," Steve Belichick said. "I told 'em it didn't matter and it wasn't a big deal. I was a man and he was a man. Simple as that. Bill was raised along those lines."

He would eventually become a leader who would work with, befriend, and earn the trust of men from all nationalities. That's part of coaching, too. It's probably just as important as holding that clicker in your right hand and knowing when to rewind, fast-forward, and stop.

"In order to do a lot of different things defensively, you have to be an outstanding teacher," Jimmy Johnson says into the telephone. "There are some decent coaches who are just OK teachers. Bill is able to teach a variety of things that a lot of coaches would either be too intimidated to teach because it's out of their comfort zone, or they just don't have the talent to do it."

Johnson, the former Cowboys and Dolphins coach, became friendly with Belichick in the early 1990s. They made a couple deals together. They saw each other at the Kentucky Derby (when you grow up in a state that Pimlico calls home, you learn to love horse racing). They respected one another's passion for football.

Last spring, Johnson invited Belichick to visit with him in Miami. The plan was for the men to fish and talk football. The weather had other plans. It was extremely windy and the two sailors didn't get the sense that they would be successful pulling in fish.

So they talked.

Belichick told Johnson that he was concerned about the number of 2003 draft picks he had with the Patriots. He didn't know if he would be able to find playing time for all the picks.

"Draft picks are like money," Johnson told him. "You can use them, you can trade them for future picks, or you can use them to acquire players."

The beauty of a good student, whether he is a football coach or not, is his ability to listen. Belichick will listen to three or four people tell him the same thing. Or similar things.

"He's a sponge," said Pat Hill, the coach at Fresno State and a former Belichick assistant. "It's amazing how much information he can absorb and then turn around and organize that information. I can't tell you how much he has helped me."

No one was sure Belichick would end up here.

He still is the kid who marked a line on his basement wall and practiced his long snapping.

He is the young man—really, he and his bride look almost the same as they did in '77—who got married under the bronzed dome of the Naval Chapel. He is the father—and the coach—who in October quietly arrived at the Dexter School in Brookline (John F. Kennedy's alma mater) and watched his youngest son, Brian, play football the way he likes it. There were no numbers or names on the jerseys. No facemasks, either.

He is the educator—Johnson calls him a "progressive teacher"—who sat in a quarterbacks meeting last season and gave an impromptu demonstration on the difference between arthritis and tendinitis. Damon Huard had casually mentioned arthritis and asked the coach a question. As Steve and Jeanette learned years ago, he had an answer.

Talking about Belichick's defensive analysis later, Tom Brady said, "He's pretty smart, huh?"

He is the economics major, golden in today's numbers-crunching NFL, who shrugs off his 715 score on the math portion of the SAT. "What's important," he once said with a laugh, "is that I know how to count to 11." If he wasn't coaching football, he said he would work with a big business for a little while before going into business for himself.

He is someone who continues to empathize with the little guy behind the scenes, because that's how he came into the league. "He walked in the NFL as a dishwasher, so to speak," Hill said, "and worked his way up." Last year, he tossed a Reebok catalogue to a few of the 20-somethings on his office staff and told them to pick what they wanted.

He remembers the days when he was a long-haired kid, sneaking off to New Orleans for Mardi Gras (his father once scared a roommate into telling him where Bill was). He remembers being pulled over by the Mississippi State Police, presumably because of his hair.

He remembers—well, no he doesn't. He doesn't remember a time when he was ever about style at the expense of substance.

"Let me ask you something," Bon Jovi said, beginning to laugh. "Have you ever seen him wear his bling-bling? Really. Have you ever seen him wear any of his Super Bowl rings?"

The answer would be no.

"You see all these old coaches wearing their rings. They could have won them in the 1970s and they're still wearing them. I work with Jaws [Ron Jaworski] and he wears his NFC Championship ring like it's his wedding band. And he won that thing 23 years ago! You're more likely to see Bill's boys wearing his ring than him."

Belichick is all about football. He is about seeing teams come together and do something significant. He is out for what the rings symbolize, not the rings themselves.

Bon Jovi has co-written a movie that has been picked up by Universal. He was asked if he wrote in a character for Belichick.

"That would be the strong, silent type," he said. "Right?"

It's a start. But it's only a small percentage of the movie.

Tom Brady

Most popular

by JACKIE MACMULLEN

The first time, it happened too fast. One day, Tom Brady was a young quarterback with no pro credentials who tried to meet women by telling them, "You know, I play for the Patriots." It never worked. The women didn't believe him, nor did the bouncers, who waved him off to the back of the line with the rest of anonymous working stiffs. Brady would shrug, grin at his pal Dave Nugent, another no-name Patriot, and wait his turn like everyone else.

Then, suddenly, frantically, he was waved to the front of the line. New England's starting quarterback Drew Bledsoe suffered a sheared chest muscle in a game against the New York Jets, and Brady was the new starter. He stepped into the job like he was slipping into an elegant, tailor-made suit. He was a perfect fit for coach Bill Belichick's offense: a cerebal, confident, natural leader.

New England won games with Brady in charge. Lots of games. Bledsoe returned, but his job was taken. Brady was careening towards stardom, the Super Bowl. Overnight, he became Boston's most desirable bachelor. He was mobbed when he bought gas, so he got in the habit of choosing full serve. He was overrun with fans at his old haunt, the Outback Steakhouse, so he started ordering take-out. Young girls knocked on his apartment to ask him to the prom, so he stopped answering the door.

By the time his team arrived in New Orleans in 2002 to play the heavily favored St. Louis Rams in Super Bowl XXXVI, Brady was tired, overwhelmed, and frustrated. He led the Patriots to a thrilling upset, collected the MVP trophy, then, like Wade Boggs before him, tried to will himself invisible.

He couldn't. He didn't. He was a top shelf celebrity, stuck with all the trappings that accompanied it.

"All the stuff that came at me two years ago, I wasn't ready for it," Brady admits now. "I didn't know how to say no. I got mad at myself when I said yes. I found myself sitting at home, afraid to go out.

"Then, when I did go out, I felt like I was dodging bullets all day. I mean, people are following you home. How do you deal with that?"

He is back again at his second Super Bowl in three years, poised to rachet up his celebrity to an even higher level. Yet the Brady who entertained the largest number of media of any player in Houston is no longer harried. He has learned to manage his new life as efficiently as he manages the Patriots offense. He has come to accept the fact he can no longer just shoot out to a movie, or grab some dinner uninterrupted. He has learned to delegate his responsibilities. And he has learned to say no.

"I think I have somewhat of an idea what I'm getting into this time," Brady said. "It got so chaotic two years ago, I found myself thinking, `When is this season going to end?' I don't feel that way this time.

"The pressure to go out and play well, the pressure to go out and win, that's there every week. I'm used to that by now."

The numbers he has submitted in critical situations are spectacular. He has a 5-0 career mark in postseason, a 7-0 overtime record, 13 fourth-quarter comebacks in three years. He did not throw an interception at home during the regular season. If Brady leads New England to victory over the Carolina Panthers, he will be the youngest repeat Super Bowl quarterback winner in NFL history.

He is already one of the most popular. The Houston Chronicle conducted a Google search with the words "New England Patrtiots quarterback Tom Brady." There were 98,600 re-

"The pressure to go out and play well,
the pressure to go out and win, that's there every
week. I'm used to that by now." TOM BRADY

sponses. The Chronicle staff then punched in "New England Patriots hunk Tom Brady." There were 119 responses. Brady is so hot, he's catapulted onto the big screen (catch him in "Stuck on You" in theaters near you). He is so hot the opposing quarterback, Jake Delhomme, wants to be him when he grows up, and he's three years older than Brady.

"The more he wins, the worse it will get," predicts Hall of Fame quarterback Joe Montana, who won 4 Super Bowls. "People love a winner. It's unfortunate, really, when you think about it, because people tend to completely forget the guys on the losing team, and many of them played pretty well."

"I do think something that needs to be looked at in general, in this country, is the lack of privacy people are afforded. You have people standing at the top of a hill from 800 yards away, and taking a picture of you on your own front porch. Why should people be allowed to do that?"

Montana had lunch with Brady during the past offseason, and shared his conversation with former Lakers star Magic Johnson about the difficulties of appearing in public.

"Magic told me this story," Montana says. "He was at an amusement park with his son, and every five feet he had to stop and sign an autograph. Finally, his son said, 'Hey, are you with them, or are you with me?' Magic got the message. He said after that, he decided if he was going to disappoint someone, it was going to be the strangers, not the people he loves."

"One thing I've learned in the last two years is I have to find time for myself," Brady agrees. "You have to do that, to keep your sanity. The other thing is you have to make sure you do are able to prepare to play football. You can't let anything else get in the way of that."

He does not want sympathy. You can't expect people to feel sorry for you when you can do what you want, whenever you want. Brady spent part of the team's week off visiting with president Bush. Two years ago, he would have thought such a possibility preposterous. Brady briefly chatted about his football team, then wished the Commander in Chief luck in the next election. Bush wished Brady luck in the Super Bowl. "He's the only guy who hasn't asked me for tickets," Brady says.

His teammates see a different player from two seasons ago. Brady was always composed, but now there's a sophistication that accompanies it.

"Tom has matured quite a bit since the last time we were here," says running back Antowain Smith. "When we were in New Orleans he was so excited he'd get in the huddle and start yelling out all the plays. I'd tell him, 'Hey, Tom, calm down. What did you just say?'"

"Tom would be in the huddle all fired up, slapping guys on the helmet," concurs offensive lineman Damien Woody. "I thought he was going to give someone a concussion."

Yet even in the midst of his first Super Bowl, Brady displayed an uncommon poise. An hour and a half before kick off of Super Bowl XXXVI, he curled up in front of his locker and took a nap. In the final seconds of the game, as the Patriots positioned themselves in field goal range, Brady intentionally spiked the ball to stop the clock. The ball bounced back up, and the he instinctively balanced the ball on his hand for a moment, before flicking it back.

"It's just something quarterbacks do sometimes," Brady says. "Like Tiger Woods hitting the golf balls on his driver."

But was it prudent to engage in such frivolity moments before the game would be decided?

"I don't know," the quarterback shrugs. "I thought we had the game pretty well in hand."

He was more naiive then. Wasn't football fun? He learned differently when his close friend, Lawyer Milloy, was released days before the season opener this year because he would not re-structure his contract. Brady was sur-

prisingly candid in expressing disappointment in the organization for cutting his friend loose. Those comments, says Brady, led to a visit from owner Robert Kraft after New England got thumped by Milloy's new team, the Buffalo Bills.

"Robert talks to me a lot," Brady says. "He has a way of looking at things differently. He's been through a lot of tough things in his own life. He came to me and said, 'I was really worried about you after that game. You seemed so angry. You weren't yourself.'

"His message was he wanted me to get over it quickly. And I did. And we turned it around."

While Kraft and coach Bill Belichick probably would have preferred Brady to keep his comments to himself, the quarterback's willingness to articulate what so many of his teammates were thinking did not go unnoticed in the lockerroom.

"Tom is the team spokesman," Woody says. "We all understand he has to pick his spots. Tom has a lot of responsibility on his shoulders. But when it came to the Lawyer thing, he had some things to get off his chest. If he had said anything different than what he did say, it wouldn't have been genuine."

The willingness to be outspoken comes with experience. If Brady is going to carry the load, he should have the right to speak about the weight of it.

"I never felt like I could say anything (my first year as a starter)", Brady confesses. "I hadn't earned it. You earn that by showing up on time, by performing consistently, but working out with the team, by putting in your time. When I see new young guys come in, and start yapping, I tell them to shut up."

If he could do something over, he would not have let his post Super Bowl commitments keep him from his annual vacation with his father. He would have shared more of his success with friends. He would have skipped some of the parties.

His time remains at a premium, but he will not let it intefere with what is truly important to him. When, for instance, offensive coordinator Charlie Weis awoke from stomach reduction surgery which initially left himcomatose, the first person he saw was his wife. The second was his young quarterback, who had kept a vigil at his bedside.

"He said, 'If I didn't come, I was afraid you were going to yell at me again,' Weis recalls. "He stayed for 48 hours. He even told my wife, 'Go. Eat.' I'll wait here."

Brady will be there for them. His coaches and his teammates know that. If he leads the New England Patriots to another Super Bowl win, he will brace for inevitable avalanche of opportunities, demands and responsibilities. If his team loses, he will lose a little luster. No matter. He has plenty to spare.

Born to stun

by MICHAEL HOLLEY

The first time Ida Law saw her 8-pound, 7-ounce grandson, she was given a glimpse of the future. She saw it so clearly, in fact, that she had to tell somebody.

"Look at him," Ida said to her daughter, Diane. "He's already a little linebacker."

This was western Pennsylvania, 1974. Steady work at a steel mill could put money in your pocket, and going to see the Pittsburgh Steelers could give you reason to spend it. Those were great days for both local industries—steel and pro football—so being associated with one usually meant something good.

Forget about the difference between cornerbacks and linebackers; Ida was correct. She was certainly staring at a football player, a player to be raised in the region that produced Tony Dorsett, Mike Ditka, Dan Marino, and Joe Montana. Nearly 30 years after Ty Law's grandmother told the world what her grandson would become, one of Law's college roommates had this to say after thinking about his friend's football life:

"Some guys were born to do what they do. I truly believe Ty was made for this."

Deollo Anderson made that comment earlier this week, based on his observations from 1992 to the present. He didn't get a chance to see the Ty Law from Wykes Street in Aliquippa, Pa. He didn't get a chance to see the little things Law did in the 1970s and '80s, little things that let people know he had a football player's instincts and a comedian's timing.

All the kids in the neighborhood knew Law was fast. Sometimes he would walk toward home and chant the name of Bullet, a dog that used to chase the kids on Wykes. As soon as Bullet would charge, Law would run, seeing if he could make it to his grandparents' front porch before the dog made it to his backside.

Law always won that race.

There were several times when one of the local men would gather the children together and give them a challenge. The man would of-

fer $1 to the child who could outrun Law all the way around the block. He knew it would never be a fair race, so the man would allow the other children a 15-second head start and see if that helped.

"Ty always beat us," said Byron Washington, Law's best friend from across the street. "I don't ever remember him losing one of those races."

There may have been someone who was faster, in a vacuum. But there wasn't anyone his age who was faster and more competitive. In football, that meant the Little Quips had two major offensive plays.

"Ty Left and Ty Right," Washington said with a laugh.

Law was good and had been that way as long as anyone could remember. He played baseball, basketball, football, and any other sport you said he couldn't play. He fished with his grandfather, who was "Paps" to all the kids on Wykes.

He was a break dancer, who would put a piece of linoleum or cardboard in the street and spin.

He took advantage of western Pennsylvania's hills and used them to train, even when he didn't have a training partner. He ran up and down the hills, and when he finished doing that he would backpedal up and down.

Sometimes he sat in his classes at Aliquippa High and wrote in the textbooks. He was practicing his autograph for the pros. He knew he would get there some day, and he and Washington talked about it all the time. Washington loved football as much as Law, but he could see that the kid wearing No. 20 for the Quips was gifted, driven, and seemingly selected to be great at something.

"Let me put it to you this way," said Washington. "He's the type of person who will not let you beat him. If you play tennis, he'll say he'll beat you at tennis. If it's swimming, he's going to outswim you. If it's running, he's going to outrun you."

It's not tennis, swimming, or road racing now. It's pro football, a place where Law always expected he would be. There was never a mo-

"Ty and Charles Woodson are the top corners
in football, hand's down. Can you name anyone else?
... Not many people can do what Ty does." ANTHONY DORSETT

ment when he lacked confidence—maybe that's why he still believes he can be a productive receiver.

(He practiced at receiver before the Patriots played the Texans on Nov. 23, but the team decided not to put him in the game.)

There was never a moment when he backed away from something he believed in or bit his tongue when there was something that needed to be said—maybe that's why he stays away from deep analysis of the Patriots' release of his friend Lawyer Milloy.

"He's honest as hell," Anderson said. "He won't sugarcoat a thing."

For Ty Law, the stage can never be too big nor the ante too excessive. AFC Championship vs. co-MVP Peyton Manning: three interceptions. The Super Bowl vs. Kurt Warner and the rams: interception return for a touchdown. He believes that he's supposed to be here.

It's as if Ida Law spoke and an 8-pound, 7-ounce boy understood every word.

During 1980s summers, Wykes Street would get a visit from another future pro. Anthony Dorsett would be in town to visit his grandmother at one end of the street. Law lived at his grandparents' house at the other end.

Dorsett and Law are cousins.

They didn't get a chance to play on any teams together—"I have moved away before that could happen," Dorsett said—but they remained close. They were both fans of the team Dorsett's father, Tony, played for: the Dallas Cowboys.

If Anthony didn't realize in the '80s that his cousin was a born football player, he knows it now.

"Ty and Charles Woodson are the top corners in football, hand's down," Dorsett said. "Can you name anyone else?"

Champ Bailey?

"Man, please," Dorsett said. "Bailey talks about himself more than anyone else does. You can't be great just because you say you are."

Chris McAllister?

"I've watched him play," he replied. "Not many people can do what Ty does."

What Law does is play man or zone coverage. He plays the run well and covers well. He can be physical at the line, surprising people who have never played against him.

"I don't know if a lot of players understand how strong he is," said Steve King, who played with Law at the University of Michigan. "If he gets his hands on you, he can totally disrupt you at the line."

Making himself more dangerous, Law has added a new level of preparation to his game. He said recently that he relied on his instincts and talent as a young corner. "And after the game," he said, "I would say to myself, 'Why am I so tired? Damn, I'm tired.'"

He learned that the combination of instincts and preparation could make his job easier. The nation saw that against the Colts in the AFC Championship Game. He knew what was coming on his first interception, so he told safety Rodney Harrison about it. During the play, he pointed to Harrison, "reminding him to take the corner post route." Harrison covered it and Law brought in a one-handed interception.

"I'm not surprised by any of it," said King, now an academic adviser in Northwestern's athletic department. "I've seen him do this his entire career.

"I always feel like he's going to make a play in a big game. I remember watching [Super Bowl XXXVI] with a bunch of people who aren't Patriots fans. I like to do that. So I was sitting there watching it when he got the pick. I knew he was going to do it. When he ran to the end zone, I said, 'Now, pat it down.' And he did."

Patting it down is part of Law's end zone dance. His family and his friends know him that well. They can almost intuit when he's going to make a play and predict what he's going to do after he makes it.

Dorsett watched the play against the Rams, too. He watched his cousin break on the ball and return it for the score. He thought Law should have been the game's MVP, not Tom Brady.

This trip to the Super Bowl is as indisputable as Law's place among the best in the game. It was just another challenge to stop the speed of Carolina's Steve Smith or the size and strength of Muhsin Muhammad.

Those who have studied Law will tell you that this is just one more challenge to add to the cornerback's considerable file.

As a freshman at Michigan, he made an impression in an early scrimmage. He was facing Derrick Alexander, who eventually became one of Bill Belichick's first-round picks in Cleveland. Alexander tried to fool him on a fade route and Law intercepted the ball. On another play, Law intercepted again.

He had caught everyone's attention. He never redshirted at Michigan.

"We all came in thinking we were top dogs," King said. "But Ty was special."

He was also funny.

Once, during a public speaking class, he decided to give his talk on safe sex. By the end of his lecture, he had everyone—the professor included—laughing. And he had come away with the highest grade.

When he and Anderson learned that they would be roommates, they talked on the phone. Soon after they met in person, Law went to work on Anderson, making fun of his tight pants. A meticulous dresser—chances are he's been inside a mall near you—he used to tell Anderson and King how sharp he looked at his high school prom.

"And then we saw the picture," Anderson said.

"You've got to ask him about it," King confirmed.

Apparently, Law wore a peach, satin suit to his prom ("I say it's pink," King said). "It looks terrible," Anderson, now a supervisor at Ford, said. "We blazed to him to no end on that, but he thought it was the sweetest thing. To this day, he'll tell you how good it looks. That's Ty."

While at Michigan, Law stayed true to the football prophecy he heard as an infant. He didn't like watching football games on television. He didn't like playing video games. He was obsessive about taking naps so he wouldn't be worn down. He liked his clothes, his hiphop and R&B, and his kung-fu movies.

He didn't like anything that got in the way of football.

"He's always been a good athlete," Diane Law said. "I think he got it from me—I was such a tomboy growing up."

Diane said she usually doesn't attend games in person because the view isn't always great and she doesn't have the luxury of instant replay. She was in New Orleans on Feb. 3, 2002, though.

"One of the most fun times of my life," she said. And then, showing that her son also gets his sense of humor from her, she added, "If you go to jail in New Orleans, you must have killed someone. Because everything else seems to be legal."

Diane Law was in Reliant Stadium for Super Bowl XXXVIII, and so was Byron Washington. After the game, the plan is for them to talk about Super Bowls, just like they did as kids.

"Ty wants to win and he wants to remain a Patriot," Washington said. "I think he can see himself in the Hall of Fame."

Richard Seymour

Prime Stopper

by JOHN POWERS

He stands soft-spoken sentinel at his dressing space just inside the entrance to the Patriots locker room. Big Sey—Richard Vershaun Seymour to his parents and the IRS—is wearing a Homeland Defense knitted cap. While it's officially disavowed by the Gillette Stadium pro shop, Tom Ridge's color-coded guardians don't seem to mind.

"Just something to have some fun with," says Seymour, but he and his fellow defenders want to make sure you don't miss their arms-crossed point. No Cowboy, no Dolphin, no Titan, and no Colt comes into the foreboding windswept mansion atop Route 1 and comes out with a victory.

"That's what it's always been," says Seymour, the masonry contractor's son. "We've gotta protect our house."

Nobody has done a better job of it than this New England bunch, which has won a club-record 10 straight (and 18 of 21) at home, allowed only four touchdowns on the premises during the regular season, and are determined to prevent their first home playoff loss since 1978.

Seymour wasn't born then (he's 24) but he's the biggest man in the building now, a 6-foot-6-inch, 310-pound colossus who is the chief disruptor along the front line of the league's stingiest defense and who's headed to the Pro Bowl for the second year in a row.

"Richard Seymour is playing a total game," attests Indianapolis coach Tony Dungy, who was hoping his offensive line can keep Seymour from totaling golden-armed quarterback Peyton Man-

"Instead of being a good defensive lineman he
wants to be one of the best, and that's what he is
right now. One of the best." TEDY BRUSCHI

ning. "He's playing against the run, rushing the passer, and playing with a lot of energy. As a coach that appreciates defensive line play, he's fun to watch."

If his listed position is a generic "defensive lineman," it's because Seymour has played all of them during this mix-and-match, plug-in-a-body season, when 20 different players started on defense, seven of them up front.

Depending on the scheme and the injured list, Seymour found himself at end or tackle, inside or outside, his next-door neighbor changing by the week. "When you come in on Wednesday to see where you're going to be playing, you'd get the task," he says.

When the season began, Seymour lined up as left end in a 3-4 defense. When nose tackle Ted Washington went down and linebackers began dropping, Seymour shifted to left tackle in a 4-3 for two games, then moved to right end in a 3-4 for another, then to right tackle for two games in a 4-3. Then it was back to right end in a 3-4 for four games before switching back to right tackle. "That's not easy," says linebacker Ted Johnson. "Taking a guy out of his comfort zone."

Not that Seymour minded. He'd expected to be the roving ambassador up front, so he wasn't hung up on being tethered to a fixed address. "When your number's called, it's time to make plays," he says. "You have to make plays."

Nobody remembers where Seymour started out when kicker Olindo Mare lined up for the field goal that figured to beat the Patriots with two minutes left in regulation in their October meeting in Miami.

All that mattered was that Seymour got his big mitt in between ball and goal post and his colleagues went on to win in overtime and end their 0-13 autumnal tropical hex. "He's a force," says Johnson. "I saw that from Day 1."

Seymour came here three years ago out of Georgia, a No. 1 draft pick (sixth overall) who was viewed as a defensive building block for a team that had lost 11 games, finished fifth in the division, and routinely gave up three touchdowns a game. "They needed a big body," he mused, a few months after his arrival. "I'm it."

Seymour quickly proved he was more than a giant slab of pre-cast concrete. His mission, from the start, was "getting off the ball and causing havoc" from whatever direction he was coming. His goals: a Super Bowl ring and an annual trip to Hawaii to consort with his All-Pro peers.

Who knew that he'd have both checked off the list so quickly?

"I couldn't have said that I would be in this position," says Seymour, who's the first Patriot defensive lineman to go to consecutive Pro Bowls since Houston Antwine in 1968.

"I knew I would be a good player, but I wasn't sure how the chips were going to fall," Seymour says. "I've definitely been blessed, for where I am in my career. Two Pro Bowls, a Super Bowl ring, and a chance to go for another. In three years, that's pretty outstanding. A lot of guys don't do that in their whole careers."

Given the longevity of defensive linemen, Seymour could be around for a decade or more. "The sky's the limit for him," says cornerback Ty Law, a fellow Pro Bowler. "Richard hasn't even reached his potential yet. That's the scary part. He's going to be the new breed of defensive lineman. I guarantee you, in two years, he's going to be the standard."

Seymour is already considered a seasoned veteran among a roomful of them, a bunch of whom have been around for a decade or more, and who've named Seymour a defensive captain. "That's an indication of the respect his teammates have for him," observes coach Bill Belichick.

Since the day he arrived, Big Sey has been a fixture on the D-line, starting all but four games that he's been available to play. Which is why his benching for last month's Jacksonville game, after Seymour missed two practice days to attend his grandfather's funeral in South Carolina, gnawed at him like a canker.

"Any time you're a captain, you want to be out there with your team," says Seymour, who was nearly in tears about what Belichick cryptically called a "coaching decision." "That was probably the toughest thing about it. You feel you're ready to go, but the opportunity isn't there. But I've always been a firm believer that coaches coach and players play."

When Seymour got in the game, he played like a dervish, making seven tackles (five solo) and clocking quarterback Byron Leftwich from the blindside to force a fumble.

"Richard's taken it upon himself to take his game to the next level," says linebacker Tedy Bruschi. "Instead of being a good defensive lineman he wants to be one of the best, and that's what he is right now. One of the best."

As the season dwindles and the stakes increase, it's all about elevated effort. The higher you go up the mountain, Seymour likes to say, the more blustery things get. And now, one game from the summit? "It's windy out there," he reports.

It's the other guys—the McGinests and Washingtons, the Bruschis and Vrabels, the Laws and Harrisons—who've stepped up to make the New England defense the NFL's most parsimonious. But Seymour is the man most likely to breach the wall first, to separate the quarterback's head from his shoulders.

Willie McGinest

The cornerstone

by JACKIE MACMULLEN

Do not lock arms with Willie McGinest and attempt a stroll down a meandering nostalgic path. Do not rhapsodize about his remarkable season, in the face of skeptics who were certain he was getting too old for this. Please, do not dwell on what might have happened, or what could have been. If it's photographs and memories you are after, trust me, you've chosen the wrong football jersey.

Concentrate on the present. That's always preferable with this fiercely proud man, who was just named to his second Pro Bowl eight seasons after he made his first. There could have been more—probably should have been—but there was a string of nagging obstacles that impeded his progress: bad hamstring, bad neck, then the knee, the other knee, the ankle, back, and groin. The groin was a real killer. That injury dogged McGinest for most of the 1998 season, causing him to miss seven games and hobble through quite a few more. When McGinest is healthy, he is one of the most fearsome players in football. But when he's not, he's like anyone else: vulnerable, limited, frustrated.

Whatever you do, do not bring up injuries to him. Bad, bad idea. His mood darkens when the subject is broached. He can't understand why it's even a topic. Don't you realize that if you play the game of football properly, occasionally your body will pay the price?

"It's a violent sport," McGinest said. "People get hurt all the time. I'm just one of those peo-

ple. But people make it seem like I'm different somehow. Why does everyone focus on my injuries?"

Perhaps because they are the only things that have been able to stop Willie McGinest. When he came to New England in 1994, the No. 4 overall pick in the draft, he was penciled in as the next Lawrence Taylor—or, at the very least, the next Junior Seau or Andre Tippett. He was tall, lean, aggressive, nasty, athletic, and versatile. He had worn the vaunted No. 55 at Southern Cal and lived up to the honor. They called him "Wild Dog" in college, and when he reported to the Patriots and began laying punishing hits on offensive teammates in practice, nobody from the staff had to ask why.

He made the Pro Bowl in his second season, 1996, as a defensive end. He collected 9.5 sacks and even had an interception, which he returned 46 yards for a touchdown. He went to the Super Bowl. His future seemed limitless.

But the injuries began pecking away at him the following year. He struggled with a hamstring pull, an injured right knee, a sprained left knee, a sprained ankle. In '98, a nagging groin injury robbed him of his explosiveness and his confidence. It was the first—but not the last—time people wondered whether McGinest would thrive in the NFL the way the Patriots hoped he would.

Well, here he is. Judge for yourself. His nickname around the league is "Old Man," and the preseason forecast for him was the usual impending doom. Young linebacker Rosevelt Colvin was coming aboard, and the blueprint

"I've never seen anyone like him. He's as almost as big as a defensive lineman. He can handle the big guys and run with the little guys" CHRISTIAN FAURIA appeared to call for McGinest to serve in a backup role at both outside linebacker and defensive end. He would have a diminished if dignified role.

But Colvin went down with a season-ending hip injury in Week 2. Plans changed.

McGinest started 11 games at linebacker. He recorded 67 tackles and 5.5 sacks. He became indispensable—again.

"I've never seen anyone like him," said Patriots tight end Christian Fauria. "He's as almost as big as a defensive lineman. He can handle the big guys and run with the little guys. I've never had to play against him, and I'm glad. He causes problems for guys like me."

You might recall the angst McGinest laid on the Indianapolis Colts the first time they met. On the final play of the game, with the Colts looking at a fourth and goal from the 1 and the game hanging in the balance, McGinest burst through the line and leveled running back Edgerrin James to end it. He celebrated by streaking up the field like an Olympic sprinter.

This caused some raised eyebrows, because two plays earlier, McGinest had gone down, stayed down for a bit, then limped off the field in apparent distress. The Colts argued that McGinest was stalling for time, allowing his defense, which had no timeouts left, a breather against the relentless Colts offense.

An inquiring Indianapolis journalist posed the question to McGinest before the rematch with the Colts in the AFC Championship game. Was he really hurt?

The Old Man's eyes narrowed. Bad idea. No questions about injuries, remember?

"My knee got caught up," McGinest answered. "For the last time—and this is the last time I am going to talk about this—I have been a player who has been involved in injuries in the past. If you have been hurt before, that is one thing you do not ever want, to jinx yourself and pretend you are hurt. Nobody wants to be hurt.

"If I was faking, I would have come back in the very next play. It took me two plays to gather myself. If the whole game comes down to that, then that's their fault for trying to run the ball at me. Maybe they should have tried something else."

"I think this year Willie put aside trying to live up to being the fourth overall pick and concentrated on just being a solid football player," said linebacker Mike Vrabel. "The way he jams receivers and disrupts plays is just unbelievable. He ping-pongs receivers and tight ends into each other.

"If you are willing to do that, you're not going to get a big contract or a whole bunch of stats, but you are going to help your team."

Clearly, Pro Bowl voters understood this.

When Ravens outside linebacker Peter Boulware gave up his Pro Bowl spot to have knee surgery, McGinest was selected as his replacement. He didn't lead the team in sacks (that was Vrabel, with 9.5), nor did he lead the team in tackles (that was Rodney Harrison, with 126), but he did enough other things that aren't represented numerically—such as jamming receivers.

"When someone does that to you, it screws your timing up," Fauria said. "For the most part, it screws the quarterback's timing up, too.

"If Willie is knocking your tight end 5 yards into the backfield, where's the running back going to go?"

When he played for the Bears, Colvin studied McGinest on film, but the Old Man was even more than he imagined in person.

"He's a vet," Colvin said. "If you look in the dictionary for the definition of the word `veteran,' you'll see Willie's picture next to it. He's a guy you can depend on."

"I'm happy for Willie," said cornerback Ty Law. "It's incredible what he's done. He's always putting pressure on the quarterback or bothering the receivers. He's made my job so much easier. I think the coaching staff decided to just let him go this year. Willie's at his best when he's roaming free.

"A lot of people said he couldn't do it anymore, but he's probably led the team in game balls, and you know [Bill] Belichick doesn't give those out freely."

McGinest's third Super Bowl seems like a lifetime removed from his second. He battled back troubles in 2001, playing in 11 games and starting only five, the fewest of his career. His role was unclear, and that pained him more than any physical malady.

"You could see it in his face," said fellow veteran Troy Brown. "It hurt him. But he didn't quit. He hung in there. Now he's on top of his game again."

McGinest had a monster sack on St. Louis quarterback Kurt Warner in the Patriots' Super Bowl win over the Rams two years ago, yet within minutes of the triumph, his future was a topic. Gossip columnists from the Boston Herald reported that McGinest was contemplating retirement.

"It was ignorant," McGinest said. "You had those two ladies from the Inside Track just throwing stuff out there, two people who know nothing about football. They had no idea what was going on with me."

Retire? No, he wasn't close to being done. McGinest returned last season and played in all 16 games. He missed two this year with nagging neck trouble, but he has been there when it mattered most—such as fourth and goal from the 1 in Indianapolis.

A perfect fit

by JACKIE MAC MULLEN

e caught the ball precisely the way it was diagrammed. Tedy Bruschi was elated. This was exactly what he'd worked toward, a big play in a big game to prove to his coach, Bill Parcells, that he belonged on this football team, that he wasn't too short, or too slight, or too young to be an impact player.

He knew Parcells had been hesitant to draft him. He was used to doubters surveying him at a shade over 6 feet, and 245 pounds, and wondering aloud how he would ever be able to rush the quarterback successfully. Bruschi wanted to play defensive end in college, but the recruiters kept politely correcting him. No, son. You won't be able to do that at the next level.

When the Arizona staff agreed to give the kid a shot at his desired position, he promised them they would never regret it. He immersed himself in the middle of a defensive crew called the "Desert Swarm," and tied the all-time Division 1A record for career quarterback sacks with 52.

The pro scouts told him again he was too small to be a defensive end, and this time, Bruschi was forced to listen. The New England Patriots drafted him in the third round, prepared to use him on special teams and specific third-down situations.

So there he was, in 1996, playing for the Patriots in a pivotal game against the Denver Broncos, and Parcells was calling for a fake punt. Tom Tupa performed his role beautifully, winding up as if to boom the ball down the field, before jerking the ball away, and tossing it to Bruschi, the rookie.

It was absolutely perfect—until Bruschi dropped the ball.

"That was the low point of my career," Bruschi said. "I had it. I had it in the bread basket, and someone knocked it out."

Defensive coordinator Al Groh groaned. He stood 8 feet away from his pupil on the sideline, tapping him on the helmet as he came off the field.

"You could see how badly it hurt him," Groh said. "It was so unusual he dropped it, because usually when you gave Tedy a job, he did it right. He took pride in that."

As he retreated to the sideline Bruschi looked up to see Parcells towering over him.

"Hold onto the ball!" Parcells growled. "Hold onto the damn ball!"

Bruschi has been in the league eight years now. He has eight career interceptions, and became the first linebacker in team history to return two interceptions for touchdowns last season. He did it again this year, including the aerial snag he made against Miami Dec. 7 that unleashed an impromptu snow shower among the euphoric Patriots fans. Bruschi also finished second in tackles (127) behind Rodney Harrison. He is not a situational player.

"He's a perpetual motion machine," fellow linebacker Ted Johnson said. "His energy is undeniable. It's always there. And he has this inner confidence."

"I'm no longer an NFL guy," said Groh, who coaches the University of Virginia, "but I've got to believe he's one of the best players in the league."

"He is someone," said defensive end Richard Seymour, "who knows how to make big plays."

He is someone who has learned how to hold onto the ball.

"I can't tell you how many times I've gone back to that play against Denver," said Bruschi. "Whenever I start feeling really good about myself, I remember that game. I remember where I came from. And I get to work again."

Bruschi is no longer underrated, underappreciated, or undervalued. He has come to symbolize the spirit and heart of this 2003 Patriots team. Unlike 2001, when New England

"Back then, you loved his attitude, and you hoped he could help you, but he's exceeded everything you could have ever expected." BILL PARCELS

stunned heavily favored St. Louis to win its first championship, the Patriots were expected to win, and players like Tedy Bruschi were expected to perform.

This is not a problem. Bruschi tackles each game, Johnson says, "with a certain joie de vivre. He loves to play."

Almost nine years ago, Groh went to the East-West college All-Star game to watch his son Michael. He left with images of Bruschi pulsating in his head.

"I was immediately intrigued by him," Groh said. "I noticed two things. The first was how everyone from the West team gravitated toward Tedy. They had only been together four or five days, but here was this bunch of All-Stars, looking to this guy as their leader.

"The second thing was his unbridled enthusiasm for the game. It was hard to miss. He performed in their practice like he was in the middle of a playoff game, and that was eye

catching."

Groh reported his findings to Parcells. Assistant coach Bill Belichick watched film of Bruschi and liked what he saw. Parcells deferred to his two respected colleagues, but still had questions about Bruschi's lack of size.

"I couldn't blame Bill," Groh said. "You looked at him, and you said, `OK, he's this height, he's this weight, where on earth would this guy work?' I wasn't sure where, but my feeling was, `Let's not dismiss him.' "

As soon as the Patriots drafted him, Bruschi identified the two daunting tasks in front of him: a new position to learn, and a new coach to convince.

"I remember the call well," said Bruschi, smiling. "The person on the phone said, `Tedy, here is Bill Parcells.' Bill got on and said, `Tedy, we're going to try you at linebacker. Here's Al Groh.' And that was it."

His first days in camp were a jumble of confusion. When the coaches told him to pick up the hook (a receiver curling into the middle of the field), Bruschi looked at him blankly. Yet he compensated for his inexperience with a plethora of other traits that Belichick quickly identified.

"He was very quick, very smart, very instinctive," Belichick said. "You can ask him to do something he's never done before, and then you watch him, and you find yourself saying, 'For a guy that's never done it, that's not bad.' So you give him something else, and he does that, too."

"You have to give Al Groh and Bill Belichick all the credit for Tedy Bruschi," Parcells said. "They saw something, and developed a role for him."

His teammates have gravitated toward him much the way they did in that college All-Star game. Bruschi was an emotional spokesman when Lawyer Milloy was released. He is the boss of a close-knit corps of linebackers. He is behind many practical jokes, including the one that left a podium strategically placed in front of linebacker Mike Vrabel's locker the day after he had a big game against Cleveland, and was summoned to the interview room.

"I knew it was Tedy," Vrabel said. "I didn't even have to ask."

Bruschi will appear in his 10th postseason game tomorrow night for the Patriots, his fifth as a starter. As he's evolved into an elite defender—one who shifted first from defensive end to outside linebacker, then last year to the inside—he has helped establish a new trend toward sleeker, smaller, quicker linebackers.

"Bill [Belichick] and I were talking about this the other day," said Parcells. "Tedy is sort of a hybrid player. Guys like him, who are versatile, dedicated, able to do different things, aren't that plentiful in this league. I've got [middle linebacker] Dat Nguyen in Dallas, but even he's a little different from Bruschi."

Nguyen is different because he played linebacker in college. Few—if any—of the other hybrid linebackers made the switch from defensive end.

"I guess that's what I sort of hang my hat on," Bruschi said. "Maybe I was one of the first so-called 'projects' that really opened the door for other guys. When the All-Pro team came out, you had [Baltimore linebacker] Ray Lewis, who is on a different level. But the other first-team guy was [Miami linebacker] Zach Thomas, and the second-team guys were me and Dat Nguyen. All three of us are a little undersized, 'I was like, [Yeah, guys, we did it.]' "

Hold onto the ball. He has come so far since then. Told that Bruschi still dwells on that play from his rookie year, Groh said the one he remembers from that season was in the AFC Championship against Jacksonville.

"It had snowed about 20 inches," Groh recalled. "Back then, [quarterback] Mark Brunell was still a pretty active quarterback. We were in a defensive scheme called 5 Robber. Because of Tedy's excellent athletic ability, and his instincts, he was the `robber.' If Brunell ran, Tedy would hunt him down. But if Brunell stayed in the pocket, Tedy was to sit back as the `robber' and try to steal anything he could in pass coverage.

"I remember the play very well. When Brunell dropped back, Tedy had his eyes fixed right on him. I just knew he was going to pick it off."

Bruschi intercepted Brunell's pass, ran it 12 yards up the field, then clutched the football close as his teammates mobbed him from the sideline. Parcells, with a hint of a smile, nodded his approval.

"That play brought some closure for me," Bruschi said. "It was in the same area of the field as the ball I dropped, right in front of our bench. When I held onto the ball, I said to myself, 'OK. Poetic justice.' "

New England was spanked by Green Bay in the Super Bowl that season. Parcells left to coach the Jets and took Belichick and Groh with him.

Would Parcells have ever guessed after his one and only year with Bruschi that the kid would turn into a second-team All-Pro linebacker?

"No, I don't think I could have ever determined that," Parcells admitted. "Back then, you loved his attitude, and you hoped he could help you, but he's exceeded everything you could have ever expected. Because of what he's done, other teams look at the Patriots and say, 'Maybe we could use a guy like Bruschi on our team.' That's the highest compliment I could give him."

Groh, who also uses a 3-4 defense in Virginia, watches the Patriots every chance he gets. He takes great delight in watching Bruschi pick off balls. Each interception reminds him of that snowy day against Jacksonville.

"Drafting Tedy was like buying a stock before it had shown a profit," Groh said. "In the personnel business, you've got to be careful about projecting someone into a totally different position. If I hadn't seen him at that East-West game, I probably wouldn't have recommended it. But anyone who has ever watched Tedy walks away saying, 'There's something about that guy.' "

Bruschi's current head coach understands. As far back as 1996, Belichick had a feeling about the brash, committed, emotional kid.

"Honestly, Tedy is the kind of guy you don't ever want to count out," Belichick said.

When he lines up against the Tennessee Titans tomorrow night, Bruschi will have his eyes fixed on Steve McNair, waiting for the moment when his instincts take hold. There may or may not be an opportunity to pick off a pass.

Hold onto the ball. Really, now. Is there any doubt he will?

The hard hitter

by RON BORGES

Rodney Harrison is a hard-edged realist when it comes to professional football. To him, these are not games being played each weekend. These are very personal confrontations in which a man measures himself or has his measure taken by another man. You win or he does.

Out of uniform, Harrison is articulate and thoughtful. He smiles freely. He can laugh about the absurdities of his business. It is not life or death to him six days a week. On the seventh day he is a violent pest, a player who is always in the same position: in your face.

That style has made Harrison a two-time Pro Bowl safety, a millionaire, and a player respected by his teammates. It has also made him a pariah to the suits who run the game from New York and diligently work to hide the NFL's violent nature while at the same time selling that aspect of it every chance they get.

Harrison is well aware of this contradiction and how it has cost him an estimated $250,000-$300,000 in fines, but he ignores that as often as he can, instead focusing on the one thing he can control: the nature of the confrontations.

Each one comes with a price. There is one for his opponent but also one for him. Limbs so sore he can barely raise his arms days later. A toll on his body that he long ago decided was worth the price, even though he understands it can be a high.

Harrison pays this price because, for him, pro football is not simply a sport. It is a nasty bit of business involving more than money. It is a business about pride and victory and who you are.

"Of course it's personal," he said. "They're trying to score touchdowns. They're trying to end your livelihood. Their success is your downfall. They don't have any love for me. You're risking everything when you go out there. Everything is serious."

This does not mean Harrison gets no joy from his sport. There is a pleasure that comes from not only survival but triumph. In Harrison's case, though, the triumphs are not defined simply by team victory. On each play—if you watch him closely—he is engaged in a more personal battle. It is one laced with violence because that is how he learned to play the game on the South Side of Chicago, where his mother, Barbara, taught him and his two siblings what life is really all about.

It took three seasons for Harrison to become a starter, but he led the Chargers in special teams tackles as a rookie and in interceptions in his second season before becoming the team's Defensive Player of the Year in 1996. He has started every game he's played since then, missing only those violent Sundays when he'd torn apart a shoulder . . . or a hamstring . . . or an ankle . . . or a few other joints and muscles. Dents come with the gladiator's life.

"I was always kind of feisty," Harrison said. "I always wanted to compete, week in and week out. I was pretty small as a kid so guys would try to pick on me. I got into a lot of fights. All the time. When I wanted to play with the bigger kids, people were always telling me I couldn't play with those bigger guys. So I fought."

And so Harrison scraped and scuffled, pushed and pulled. He got knocked down. He got up. He knocked someone down. More and more, he went down less and less. Eventually a style developed that his mother could be proud of.

It was not chippy and it was not cheap. It was confrontational. Harrison plays football in a way that defies human nature. He runs into confrontations.

"Every time someone pushes you, you have to push back," Harrison explained when asked why he seems so constantly involved in mini-sparring sessions. "You're not going to let a guy push you without pushing back. If he gets the best of me, I acknowledge it and let him know I'm coming back. I'll be there all day. The fact is, this is a physical game and the guy who's the most physical wins.

"We play a lot of different schemes and looks, and you have to know your job and complete your responsibilities but you can only deceive and confuse to a certain point. Then it comes down to football. Football is one-on-one battles. It all comes down to who's going to hit the other guy in the mouth the hardest."

Few people who play against the Patriots have any question about whom that is.

"Of course it's personal. They're trying to score touchdowns. They're trying to end your livelihood. Their success is your downfall." RODNEY HARRISON

Playing it straight

by MICHAEL SMITH

It wasn't all that long ago that the Patriots were the only team in the league whose best player was its kicker. Now, after the worst regular season of his career, which happened to coincide with the best season in franchise history, Adam Vinatieri, he of three unforgettable field goals the last time New England won the Super Bowl, was close to become something of a forgotten man. You could even argue that Vinatieri had lost his undisputed best-in-the-league belt to Indianapolis's Mike Vanderjagt.

But that was the regular season. As New England has come to learn, when the weather turns bad and games are win-or-go home, Vinatieri is always on target. He kicked the game-winner to beat the Titans in the biting cold and wind in the playoff opener. Against the Colts in the AFC Championship game, he tied and NFL record with five field goals in the snow.

It didn't look for a while as if more good fortune would await Vinatieri in pro football's second season. The first one was rough from the start, as 2003 began with Vinatieri's 110-game scoring streak coming to end in Buffalo. A year after converting a league-high 90 percent of his field goals and earning his first Pro Bowl selection, he missed nine field goal attempts during the regular season (out of 34), the most he's missed in a season, and tied for the third-most missed field goals in the league. His .735 success rate was easily the worst of his career and the third-lowest among full-time kickers in the AFC. Vinatieri began the year as the fifth-most accurate placekicker in league history. He ended it 10th.

Vinatieri had a couple of other successful runs end, as well. His streak of 33 consecutive made field goals from 40 yards and closer ended Oct. 5 against Tennessee, New England's opponent tomorrow night in an AFC divisional playoff at Gillette Stadium. He missed two field goals in that first meeting with the Titans, giving him three misses in succession for just the second time in his career.

He went an inexplicable 9 for 17 from 30 yards and beyond for the year. On Nov. 23 at Houston, Vinatieri missed for the first time in his career indoors after making 30 straight. He also hit his only game-winner of the season that day, the first time since '97 he won "only" one game with a field goal in the closing moments.

He did have his moments, however, such as accounting for all of the Patriots' 9 points in an Oct. 26 home win over the Browns and making a key 46-yarder before halftime at Denver Nov. 3.

Is that being picky? Probably. But we're talking about the only kicker to win a Super Bowl on the game's final play, one who made perhaps the most difficult kick in history, 45 yards through a blizzard in the '01 divisional playoffs against Oakland. He's set the standard pretty high. He's the Tiger Woods of placekickers.

"That's OK," Vinatieri said. "I hope people expect me to make things. I expect it of myself."

Vinatieri doesn't just look like a "real" football player, he thinks like one. To him his season was a success because the Patriots won 14 games. "[There's] room for improvement," he acknowledged. "We've had some interesting things happen throughout the course of the year. As long as our team wins. [Bill] Parcells said statistics are for losers. I like that saying, because as long as we continue to win, that's ultimately the most important thing."

Vinatieri's struggles haven't been all his fault. He went a week without his friend and holder, punter Ken Walter, who was released then re-signed. His long-time long snapper, Lonie Paxton, was lost for the season to a knee injury in Week 14. Paxton's replacement, Sean McDermott, suffered a season-ending shoulder injury in his only game. Brian Kinchen handles the snapping duties now.

Kinchen is impressed by the way the kicker has handled the transition. "There's a lot of kickers who are very finicky about snaps and holds and stuff," Kinchen said. "Adam's not like that. If it's on the tee, he's going to hit it."

"He's probably got the most respect for a kicker out of any I've ever met," said tight end Christian Fauria, who blocks for Vinatieri's field goals. "Or he's getting the most respect out of me, maybe I should put it that way. "That's the most comfortable I'm feeling, when he's back there. I don't care who's going to the Pro Bowl or how many kicks they haven't missed, he's still the guy."

Mike Vrabel

Ideal Patriot

by BOB RYAN

The New England Patriots are said to be hard-working, versatile, intelligent, self-effacing, single-minded in pursuit of victory, and, cost-efficient. Mike Vrabel is all these things. Mike Vrabel is the quintessential New England Patriot.

He is not a star. Offensive coordinators do not spend time obsessing about Mike Vrabel. It is very unlikely any opposing coach has ever spiced up a meeting by saying, "Goldangit! We've got to account for that Vrabel guy!"

In case Mike Vrabel didn't know who he was supposed to be, the national media is always around to remind him. One such account following the AFC Championship game against Indianapolis saw it this way: "There were occasions when the unheralded Vrabel, a defender of modest skills, who has been put into positions by [Bill] Belichick and [Romeo] Crennel to be effective," etc., etc., etc.

Among the "modest" skills possessed by this 28-year-old, 6-foot-4-inch, 261-pound linebacker are the ability to line up in a three-point stance and act as a surrogate defensive lineman, the ability to play the run from his linebacker spot, and the ability to play the pass from his linebacker spot. His flexibility is one of the keys to the Patriots' defensive success.

But Vrabel's ultimate value to the Patriots may be his sheer intelligence. According to an inpeccable Patriots source, that an in-house analysis of his play in 2001 revealed Vrabel to have made no, as in zero, mental mistakes during the entire season.

The Mike Vrabel story may tell you all you need to know about how the Patriots have gotten where they are. At the conclusion of the 2000 season, they made signing him one of their goals, even though he had played four years in Pittsburgh and had never started a game.

"Bill [Belichick] said, 'We've been watching you enough. We think you'll be able to help us,' Vrabel recalls. "Now I had been a decent linebacker for the Steelers, but I had never been a starter. And I guess I came in at the right price."

In the eyes of both Belichick and vice president of player personnel Scott Pioli, Vrabel was the right everything. He was part of a free agent signee class that included linebacker and special teams whiz Larry Izzo and defensive end Anthony Pleasant, who are still with the team, and guard Joe Panos and fullback Marc Edwards, who aren't. Said Pioli at the time, 'Philosophically, the team we're trying to build is a big, strong, fast, tough, smart, competitive team with reliable people . . . We're going after players that fit our system and our overall philosophy. Some people term that 'second tier' or the 'next level.' We don't see them as that type of player. They're the right player for the way we want to construct our team."

Belichick himself said, simply, that Vrabel was the kind of player who "gets it."

Vrabel was a 1997 Steelers' third-round pick out of Ohio State, where he had established Buckeye career records for sacks (36) and tackles for losses (66). He joined a very solid Pittsburgh team that had gone 53-27 in the previous five years, and that was a year removed from a visit to the Super Bowl. Among the team's acknowledged strengths was at outside linebacker, where coach Bill Cowher had the likes of Jason Gildon and Greg Lloyd at his disposal.

But Vrabel did get some playing time, and he was on the field at a critical juncture of a playoff game between the Steelers and Patriots at the end of his rookie season. With the Steelers protecting a 7-6 lead, Vrabel sacked Drew Bledsoe, shaking him loose from the football with 1:50 left. Gildon recovered, and the Steelers ran out the clock. In keeping with the whole Dangerfieldian nature of Vrabel's career, the official NFL Postseason Media Guide informs its readers that this vital sack was executed by "Mark" Vrabel.

That might bother some people, but it would only amuse Vrabel, who does not play football in order to see his name in headlines or lights. It seems he has come to the right place.

"Guys really are hungry here," he says. "Guys want to make plays. Guys are unselfish."

No one fits the profile of the Ideal Patriot more than Mike Vrabel.

"It's nice to be more than just a reserve linebacker in Pittsburgh," he says.

That's as close to preening as Mike Vrabel is ever going to get.

REFLECTIONs Tedy Bruschi Jr. and Sr.